READY TO PLAY

mental training for
student-athletes

Ron Chamberlain, Ph.D.

Sport Psychologist

Ready to Play:
Mental Training for Student-Athletes
by Ron Chamberlain, Ph.D.

Published by
Ready to Play
1133 Columbia Lane
Provo, UT 84604 U.S.A.
1-877-845-3592
www.thepsychologyofsports.com

design by Duff Tittle
photography by Mark Philbrick and Jaren Wilkey (except where noted)
copy editing by Brett Pyne
printed by University Press, Brigham Young University

ISBN 0-9742346-0-5
LCCN: 2003094227

Printed in the United State of America
  10 9 8 7 6 5 4 3 2 1

READY TO PLAY

table of contents

ACKNOWLEDGMENTS

What a thrill it has been to be a sport psychologist in a university athletic department. Every day I have the opportunity to interact with administrators, coaches, and student-athletes who have dedicated their lives to excellence. I would not have been able to write this book without the valuable experiences I have gained while working at Brigham Young University. The coaches and student-athletes have allowed me to enter their world of collegiate performance and participate in their mental training program. I have learned a great deal through my daily interaction with these wonderful people.

I would also like to thank Dr. Keith Henschen, who has been a mentor to me in the field of sport psychology; Lisa Moses, Camie Wangsgard, and Tom Golightly for their editorial support; Mark Philbrick and Jaren Wilkey for allowing me to use their outstanding photographs; Duff Tittle and Brett Pyne for designing and editing the book. Each of these individuals has made a significant contribution and helped me present my ideas more effectively.

In addition, I express gratitude for my mother- and father-in-law, Marjean and Wilford Moses. They have been a blessing in my life and have offered emotional, editorial, and financial support to this project. My mother, Kathy Chamberlain, continues to believe in me and always encourages me to take risks so my dreams can become a reality. My children, Melisa, Quinton, Emily, Amanda, and Natalie remind me what is most important and give me the energy and enthusiasm to live each day more fully. Finally, my sweet wife Jeannie, for loving me unconditionally and sharing her life and talents with me.

PREFACE

It has been a thrill for me to work as a sport psychologist with collegiate student-athletes since 1996. I am so appreciative of the athletes and coaches at Brigham Young University who have allowed me to enter their world of high-level performance. Through my experience, I have become even more convinced that mental preparation is critical for success in any athletic endeavor. I am often asked, "What is sport psychology and how can it help me as an athlete or a coach?" The purpose of this book is to succinctly answer these very questions.

The book is divided up into three main sections. First, I identify and describe what I believe are the building blocks for success. Serious athletes and coaches will recognize these building blocks as basic principles for successful living. Those who understand these principles and seek to implement them in their lives will lay the foundation for successful performance.

In the second major section, I deal with the topic of mental readiness. That is where the title "Ready to Play" comes from and is what makes this book unique. I believe there are three keys to mental readiness: activation, emotion, and focus. My objective is to help athletes and coaches to be more aware of how their activation levels, emotional states, and ability to concentrate effect their performance.

In the last major section, I describe some mental training tools athletes and coaches can use to better control their mental readiness. These tools are practical skills that can be improved with regular practice. Thus, as athletes and coaches know the building blocks for success, understand what it means to be "Ready to Play," and have some mental training skills to help them prepare, they can take control of their mental game and improve the likelihood for successful performance.

I have purposely written this book in a concise manner. There are other sport psychology books available that are more theoretical and comprehensive. However, it is my hope that student-athletes and coaches will find this book simple to read and practical to apply. It is designed to be a handy resource book that can be carried in a sports bag and referred to often to improve self-awareness and fine-tune the mental game.

I strongly believe striving for excellence is a life-long process, and that good education and regular evaluation keeps us moving in the right direction. *Ready to Play: Mental Training for Student-Athletes* is written to educate athletes and coaches about the key aspects of mental preparation and give them an opportunity to evaluate how they are progressing. Those who read the book and practice the principles and skills taught will perform at consistently higher levels of performance.

journal exercises

One of the keys to success is self-awareness. A great way for athletes to improve their self-awareness is to write about their experiences and share them with others. Throughout this book, the readers will have many opportunities to write their experiences on a variety of topics. I strongly encourage readers to take some time and complete the journal exercises throughout the book. It might also be helpful to share what you learn about yourself from these experiences with a trusted teammate, coach, friend, or sport psychologist. Remember self- awareness is the first step to change and growth.

FOREWORD

When Dr. Ron Chamberlain asked me to write this foreword, I gladly agreed. Dr. Chamberlain has helped my team members realize their potential by following the principles set forth in *Ready to Play: Mental Training for Student-Athletes.*

I asked Dr. Chamberlain to work with my Women's Cross Country Team several years ago because he is skilled at helping people excel. His love for helping people is the reason he has written this book. The results of his effort have been remarkable.

Since the inception of Dr. Chamberlain's work with the Brigham Young University Women's Cross Country Team, we have dominated the competition at NCAA National Championships, winning four out of the last six titles and finishing second on the other two occasions. I give Dr. Chamberlain a large share of the credit for this achievement; there is a direct correlation between the principles applied in our sport psychology protocol set up by Dr. Chamberlain and our team success. We think so much of his ability to help out our team that we include him in our travel party for the National Championships.

He meets with my team every Monday at the start of practice to schedule individual appointments with team members and listen to my concerns. His protocol really works. The student-athletes have the utmost confidence in him and I would not consider a season without his help. It has always been my belief that races are won first in the mind and in the heart before they can be won on the course or on the track. The imagery exercise we use in preparation for Nationals is so effective that our runners have a significant advantage going into the race. Our athletes are simply able to relax and "let it happen" during competition.

College life can be a stressful time for student-athletes. Emotion does effect performance. Learning to manage anxiety or "keeping the butterflies in formation" is vital. Confidence, through positive self-talk and imagery, and trust in the coach are essential ingredients for success. Every coach and every team can benefit by reading this book and applying the principles found within. The book is a must read for those coaches and student-athletes wishing to realize their full potential. I give *Ready to Play: Mental Training for Student-Athletes* the highest possible endorsement.

Patrick Shane
Head Women's Cross Country Coach
Brigham Young University
Three-Time National Coach of the Year

ABOUT THE AUTHOR

Dr. Ron Chamberlain has been providing sport psychology services for the Brigham Young University Athletic Department since 1996. He received his Doctoral degree in Counseling Psychology and his Masters degree in School Psychology from BYU.

He is a licensed Psychologist in the state of Utah and Certified Consultant through the Association for the Advancement of Applied Sport Psychology. He is also listed in the United States Olympic Committee Sport Psychology Registry, which is a directory of qualified sport psychology specialists. He is currently a member of the American Psychological Association (APA) and the Association for the Advancement of Applied Sport Psychology (AAASP).

Prior to his appointment in the BYU Athletic Department, Dr. Chamberlain worked in the counseling centers at BYU, Utah Valley State College, and the University of Wyoming. In addition, he worked for three years as a School Psychologist in the state of Utah. He currently maintains a part-time private practice in sport psychology.

Dr. Chamberlain grew up in Steamboat Springs, Colorado, where he competed in baseball, wrestling, track and field, football, and basketball. He earned All-State honors in basketball in 1982 and 1983. He was a three-year starter on the Mesa State College basketball team and was named to the Academic All-Conference and All-District Basketball teams. In 1989, he was named the Mesa State College Scholar-Athlete of the Year.

Dr. Chamberlain is married to Jeannie Moses and they are the parents of Melisa, Quinton, Emily, Amanda, and Natalie. His hobbies include athletics, reading, the performing arts, and family outings.

introduction

"Enjoy the little things, for one day
you may look back and realize they
were the big things."
– Robert Brault

I t was a cold winter evening in January of 1982. However, inside the gymnasium at Steamboat Springs High School, the atmosphere was electric. The Glenwood Springs Demons had come to town undefeated and ranked No. 1 in the state of Colorado.

The surprise team in this early season matchup, the No. 3 ranked Steamboat Springs Sailors, had come into the season trying to rebuild with a group of inexperienced players. They had already snuck up on some highly ranked teams in their early season tournament and beaten the league's top team on the road. Tonight would be the true test. No more would they be able to surprise the teams they played. Both teams had a couple of weeks to prepare for the game. The high school gym was packed with fans eager to cheer on their teams.

A couple of memories come to mind as I recall this memorable experience. Prior to the game, the Glenwood Springs coach complemented me on my early season success. This enhanced my confidence, which was already extremely high because I had paid my dues during the summer months by playing basketball eight hours a day. I remember the feelings of excitement, enjoyment, and optimism as game-time approached. I was so charged up for the game I felt like I was going to jump out of my skin during the introductions of the players as I watched the crazy fans waving a huge Steamboat Sailor's flag from the top row of the stands over the basketball court.

Then came the start of the game. Our coach had drawn up a play in which I would come off a double screen and shoot a 15-foot shot from the baseline. We executed the play perfectly, but due to my high activation level my 15-foot shot went about 20-feet. Fortunately, after the first few minutes of the game, the hype wore off and we executed the game plan to perfection.

My next vivid memory was getting fouled in the closing seconds of the game and looking up at the scoreboard in disbelief as we had built a 25-point lead. In a post-game interview, I was asked about what I was thinking and how I felt during my 31-point performance. The question surprised me in two ways. First, I was totally unaware I had scored my career-high until the question was asked. Second, I had few memories of how I felt or what I thought about during the game. I had experienced one of those rare "flow" experiences where everything just came together. My focus was so perfectly locked-in on each second of the game that little, if any, thinking about the game occurred until the game had concluded. The peace and fulfillment I experienced following that game was the result of good coaching, many hours of hard work, and good mental preparation. On that glorious night, I was ready to play!

journal exercise 1

Write in detail about a peak performance when you were truly "Ready to Play." What was unique about that performance?

Years later, I can examine this experience through different eyes. I am currently the Sport Psychologist at Brigham Young University. In this role, I have had the opportunity to work with hundreds of athletes from a wide variety of sports. It has been my privilege to work closely with individuals and teams who have won national championships, athletes who have earned All-American honors, and some who now make a living playing professionally. I have learned from some outstanding coaches and highly successful athletes about what does and does not work in preparing athletes to perform their best. While I do not claim to have all the answers, I do believe that I have a simple and straightforward approach that will assist coaches, athletes, and teams as they strive for excellence.

Before I begin, let me explain why I chose the title "Ready to Play" for this book. Readiness is the key to success in any endeavor. True and lasting success is never an accident. It has become very apparent to me that the national champions, All-Americans, and Academic All-Americans prepare themselves differently than the average student-athletes. They have a clear idea about what they want to accomplish and they live their lives with purpose and direction. Not everyone is willing to pay the price necessary to earn success. (Many people get excited about a goal they have set, but have difficulty sustaining the excitement, commitment, and discipline required for the highest levels of achievement.) Thus, readiness at performance time is largely determined by how people live their lives on a day-to-day basis.

Another type of readiness deals with those last few hours leading up to the performance. We have all witnessed performers who have spent years preparing themselves equally as well as the champions. Unfortunately, they fall short when it comes time to perform in pressure situations. I certainly do not see these performers as failures. Sometimes they just get bad breaks or are beaten by an athlete or team who is simply better than them on a given day. It is not always about poor mental preparation! However, there are times when performers miss opportunities to make their dreams come true because they lose their focus prior to or during major competitions and fail to manage their emotions or activation levels at critical times. To perform at a consistently high level and have those major breakthroughs,

athletes need to have skills they can use to create and maintain a game-time readiness. This type of readiness centers around three key abilities. The ability to stay focused, maintain a positive emotional state, and create an activation level that enhances performance.

The second part of the title is "to play." I recently had a college football player talk with me about an experience he had while watching his young nephew play in a pee-wee football game. He said, "I have forgotten how much fun it can be to play football." He commented on how the kids were smiling, laughing, and obviously having a good time. This experience inspired him to examine why he was no longer enjoying his sport the way he had in the past.

Serious athletes have some unique challenges. Excellence in sport requires a year-round commitment. There is tremendous pressure put on coaches and athletes to win. The intensity required to excel can lead to burnout, over-training, and boredom. There is also the reality that every aspect of the training program is not fun. Many days it is simply hard work. However, if athletes have a dream they are actively pursuing, remain intrinsically motivated, and have a support system that both challenges and encourages them, they can find great satisfaction as they journey toward their desired goals.

At performance time, athletes who simply "play the game" and focus on the process generally have more fun and achieve better outcomes than those who are pressured by themselves or others to achieve some preset standard. Successful athletes seek to win every time they perform, but they also keep their sport in perspective and maintain their child-like enthusiasm while competing. These athletes remember they are "playing a game."

journal exercise

Share your earliest memories about your participation in athletics. What and who made it enjoyable? What made you want to keep pursuing it? How did you feel while you were participating?

chapter 2

building blocks for success

"The man who moves a mountain
begins by carrying away
small stones."
– Chinese Proverb

Think for a moment about those individuals who are the most successful athletes in your particular sport. Have you ever wondered why they are the best? What makes them unique or different from everyone else? Part of it can certainly be attributed to God-given physical ability. Face it, some people are born with physical gifts like speed, strength, size, agility, and cognitive skills that set them apart from their peers. It might also be argued that they have had a different upbringing than the average person. We have all heard the story of how Tiger Wood's father, Earl, introduced him to golf as a toddler and provided an environment in which Tiger seemed destined to greatness.

While heredity and environment certainly do matter, there are other factors that are equally important. Otherwise, how would you explain the gold medals won

by Kristi Yamaguchi and Wilma Rudolph, who were born with physical dis-
abilities, and Bo Jackson, who grew up in extreme poverty and had a severe
stuttering problem as a child? There are many examples in sports of individuals who succeeded far beyond what the so-called experts would predict
possible.

photo by Duff Tittle/AJGA

I had a professor in graduate school who used an analogy to describe the interaction of heredity and environment. He compared our genetic endowment to a bucket. We are all born with different size buckets on a variety of attributes such as intelligence, strength, and speed. The bucket represents our potential on each attribute. How close we come to fulfilling our potential, or filling our bucket, is determined by our environmental conditions and life experiences.

For example, imagine twin boys are born with great athletic ability, and are separated at birth and raised in different homes. Jimmy is raised by parents who are artistic and musical and expose their children to experiences that will help them develop those talents. Jake, on the other hand, has parents who encourage him to pursue athletics. Jake's older siblings all play sports and include him at a young age. Jake will obviously have more opportunity to develop his athletic ability.

When the two boys go to college, Jake and Jimmy both arrive on the same campus. Jimmy becomes interested in sports and plays on the intramural teams. He performs quite well because of his natural ability and makes rapid improvement. Jake, on the other hand, is already on an athletic scholarship and continues to improve as he works with expert coaches. Jake's bucket is already quite full at this point. Jimmy's bucket is filling fast, but he is behind in his development when compared to Jake and may never catch up.

Other students on this same campus have been born with smaller buckets, with regards to athletic talent, and even through good coaching and experiences will never reach the talent level of Jake. Thus, a person's talent level as an athlete is greatly influenced by genetic make-up and life experiences. There are, however, another set of variables athletes themselves can control that determine, to a large degree, just how successful they can become. I call these variables the building blocks for success and each will be described in more detail in this chapter.

BIG DREAMS

Dr. Bob Rotella summed this characteristic up beautifully in his book *Golf is not a Game of Perfect*[1]. He stated, "A person with great dreams can achieve great things." I have had this statement validated many times in my work with athletes, coaches, and athletic teams.

The great ones seem to have a clear and vivid image of what they are seeking to accomplish. Their dreams are exciting, motivating, and most importantly, meaningful. They know what they want to accomplish and why it is so important to them. The reasons vary from person to person, but generally center around making a contribution to someone or something. For example, I have heard many athletes say their driving motivation to succeed in athletics has been to help their family out of poverty. Others have said, "I owe it to my coach for believing in me and giving me an opportunity to get an education."

The women's cross country team at Brigham Young University won four national championships over a six-year period. I have learned a lot about success from Coach Patrick Shane and the outstanding young women on his team. While participating in their mental preparation for the national championship races, I was impressed by the comments made by those preparing to run the race. (They seldom discussed winning nationals as their primary goal. Instead, their focus was on each person running their best race at nationals.)

The mind-set that impressed me most was illustrated in a statement made by one runner who said, "I will do my best because I know my teammates are doing their best for me." The themes of "Trust," "More Than Myself," and "No One Can Take Your Place" were used by these teams as they made final preparations for the national championship races. These themes were more than rallying slogans. The athletes internalized these themes and made them the primary reason they would excel at the championship race.

This experience taught me a valuable lesson. [People will often do more for others than they will do for themselves.] When there is a social interest, people seem to be able to dig a little deeper and find a way to perform closer to their true potential.

One of the first areas of discussion when I consult with athletes as a sport psychologist is to have the athlete share their vision about what they want to accomplish and why it is important to them. I learn a lot about the athlete in our first visit. Invariably, those who are most successful need little follow-up from the initial question. They are able to describe their vision in detail and explain why it is important to them. Many athletes are realistic with their dreams, and few have told me that they expect to be the next Michael Jordan.

One runner I worked with early in my career was getting ready to enter his senior year. He dreamed about finishing his collegiate career by running fast enough at nationals to be named to the All-American team. In addition, he had aspirations of finishing his bachelors degree and getting accepted into medical school. He was recently married and wanted to pursue his career so he could provide well for his family. The driving force in his running was to do it for his father, who had introduced him to running

at a young age and had supported him throughout his running career. As I sat and listened to this student-athlete, I got excited as he passionately described the year he was about to live.

Years later, he has accomplished all of the dreams he had discussed with me in my office with one exception. He had some health problems during his senior season that prevented him from achieving his All-American goal. He made the best of the situation, ran at nationals, and moved on to bigger and better things. Simply having dreams does not guarantee success, but failing to dream big is the recipe for mediocrity.

---

journal exercise **3**

Discuss your dreams for the upcoming year. What do you desire to accomplish? What character qualities do you want to develop or improve? What type of person do you want to be? What are the primary reasons "why" you want to pursue this dream?

BELIEF IN YOURSELF

Athletes generally use the word "confidence" to describe how much they believe in themselves. I commonly hear expressions like, "I just didn't have any confidence going into the last game because I have been practicing so poorly," or "My confidence was soaring after I made my first three shots." There are two main factors that seem to have a direct impact on an athlete's confidence. The first is good preparation. The most confident athletes have spent years developing their talents and have physically and mentally prepared themselves for the demands of their sport. Athletes who have worked hard to prepare themselves for an upcoming competition have also earned the right to feel confident. The same thing takes place in team sports when coaches have thoroughly prepared their teams and have a game plan that has been well rehearsed. It is easier to be confident when you know you are ready to perform.

The second factor that impacts an athlete's confidence level is success. It is natural for an athlete who has experienced regular success to feel more confident. Athletes who have repeatedly experienced success like Tiger Woods, Michael Jordan, and Marion Jones have an abundance of experiences to draw upon when they need a confidence boost. The recency of the success is also important. If you hit a game-winning shot in the game last night, and you have a similar situation tonight, you are likely going to feel confident when the coach draws up the play for you to shoot the final shot. It seems easier to believe in yourself if you have previously experienced success. Thus, confidence is greatly influenced by an athlete's preparation and his or her previous successful experiences. The people who end up living their dreams are those who believe in themselves and their ability to excel.

Other factors that influence the belief in self include a person's self-talk, images of success, and support from others. I met with a track runner a few years ago who had qualified for indoor nationals. She and I had met previously before major competitions to discuss her race plan and ways in which she could get mentally prepared. She was more nervous than usual for this race because she had one of the fastest qualifying times. However, she felt scared and doubted she could really compete with the best runners in the nation. She knew them by name and had looked up to them as a younger runner. She was now becoming one of them, but had put them up on a pedestal. Through her self-talk, she had convinced herself she was not capable of beating them. However, after our visit, she was able to challenge and change her self-talk, picture herself beating them, and had received a vote of confidence from myself and, most importantly, her coach. She ran a good race at nationals and received All-American honors. Even more importantly, she learned through her experience that she had arrived and could beat anyone she competed against at the collegiate level. She eventually became a national champion and has continued to excel professionally.

I share this story to illustrate a couple of key points regarding belief in yourself. First of all, it is a dynamic process. An athlete's confidence level is always fluctuating based upon his or her experiences and interpretation of those experiences. This runner needed to experience a certain level of success running against her All-American peers before she fully believed she belonged with them. Again, there is no substitute for good preparation and successful experiences. However, athletes must learn to set the stage for those successful experiences. They can do this through mental training techniques such as self-talk and imagery, which will be discussed later in this book. Furthermore, many athletes who have trouble believing in themselves will listen to a credible coach who believes in them. Coaches have a great impact on the confidence level of their athletes and can be instrumental in shaping their belief system. This runner, who won the national championship, demonstrated what can happen when an athlete dreams big and believes in herself. These are the foundational building blocks for any athlete's success.

One key attribute I have observed in people who believe in themselves is optimism. Optimistic people see opportunities and possibilities. They are full of hope, passion, and enthusiasm. These individuals bounce back quickly from mistakes, losses, and adversity. They are persistent, resilient, and mentally tough. It is enjoyable to be around optimists because they are positive and energetic. Their outlook on life is refreshing and contagious. When faced with roadblocks, they become more determined than discouraged. True optimists will not allow other people or circumstances to determine their future for them. They understand an important truth. They are the masters of their own destiny.

Recently, I had a student-athlete challenge my concept of belief in yourself. I will be forever grateful for our long discussions on this topic. Her main objection was the emphasis on the self. When taken to an extreme, the focus on the self can lead to a selfish, lonely existence where our interdependence on others is not properly understood. To me, belief in yourself must be considered within the broader context that includes family, coaches, teammates, teachers, and others. Humble athletes with good relationships seek to surround themselves with others who believe in them and support them as they pursue their dreams. They understand their success is not a glorification of the self, but a blessing from God and a team effort of many people who taught and supported them along the way. No one achieves the highest levels of success all by themselves. Therefore, belief in yourself can be summed up in the following way, "I know I can accomplish my dreams through my dedicated effort and the assistance of competent people who also believe in me and want me to succeed."

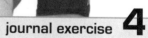

journal exercise 4

Describe a time when your confidence soared. What fed your confidence on that occasion? Who helps inspire confidence in you? What do they do or say that makes such a difference for you?

PLAN OF ATTACK

Rick Pitino introduced the idea of having an organized plan of attack in his best-selling book *Success is a Choice*[2]. Like Rick, I too have had the experience of talking with many people about their life plans and have seen a wide variety of responses to the question, "What do you want to do with your life?" You can tell a lot about a person by how they answer this simple question. Successful people are generally able to answer this question without too much thought. They seem to have a vision of where they are going and how they are going to get there. In my role as sport psychologist, I work with young adults. It is a normal developmental stage for people this age to make important decisions about what they value, how they want to contribute to society, and what career they want to pursue. It is also the age where decisions about relationships and family plans are made. It can be an exciting, yet stressful time of life to be faced with the opportunity to make so many choices. Sometimes the best plan of attack for young adults is to take some time and explore all of their options so they can make good decisions about their future.

A plan of attack is nothing more than a mental road map of where you are heading with your life. The plan is based on a person's dreams and opportunities currently available to them. These plans are not set in stone and can be changed at any time. There are a variety of reasons why a person may change his or her plan of attack. First, dreams change. What is important to a person at one point in life may change as a person ages and has new life experiences. It would seem ridiculous to continue pursuing an old dream that you no longer feel passionate about. Especially if it has been replaced by another course of action which brings excitement and enthusiasm. I have worked with many athletes who had big dreams about where their sport would take them when they arrived at college. After a year or two of college athletics, many athletes get equally excited about their majors, career plans, or relationships and that becomes their main priority instead of sports.

One of the foundational building blocks is to dream big. Dreams are nothing more than fantasies about what you would like to experience in your life and knowing why it would be important to do so. The plan of attack is a personal contract with yourself. In the plan of attack, you verbalize what it is you want to accomplish and how you are going make it happen. For example, when I began my sophomore year of college, I knew I wanted to major in psychology and play three more years of basketball. In addition, I planned to go to graduate school and get an advanced degree in psychology so I could work as a counselor. I was interested in this profession so I could help people and gain more insight into why people behave the way they do. That was my plan of attack.

I immersed myself into the life of a student-athlete and set yearly goals that would allow my plan to come to fruition. At the end of my sophomore year, I met a beautiful young woman and we began dating. By the end of the summer, we knew we would get married. We dated for another year and then got married prior to the start of my senior year. This major change strengthened my resolve to graduate on-time and get into graduate school as soon as possible. Unfortunately, I did not get into graduate school right away and my wife and I had our first child. Financial pressures began to build and I was forced to re-evaluate my plan of attack. After much thought and exploration, we decided to continue to pursue my original plan. A year later, I was accepted into graduate school at BYU and charted my course of study for the next five years. During that time, we had four more children, one of which had serious health problems as an infant and died when she was 19-months old. We moved five times in six years, served two internships, and endured the writing of my dissertation. Finally, in 1996, ten years from the time I first created my plan of attack, I was able to fulfill my educational dreams and begin a career I love. I could not have done it alone. My wife, family, and Heavenly Father made it possible for me to succeed. As I am in the beginning stages of my professional career, I now have new dreams and plans that will help me continue to move forward in my life.

This experience has taught me the importance of dreaming big, believing in myself, and having a detailed plan of attack to follow. This plan was such a part of me that I did not need to write it down. I was passionate about achieving my desires and that motivated me and gave me strength and energy. Those close to me knew my plans because I needed their support and encouragement. I prayed regularly for help, especially during the dark and challenging times. My plan of attack gave me direction and helped me to set daily, weekly, and annual goals. Every little success strengthened my confidence and gave me hope that I was going to make it. Thus, having a plan of attack is critical to any success. The vision precedes the victory.

journal exercise **5**

In journal entry 3, you wrote about a dream you have. Take some time now to write a plan of attack about <u>how</u> you are going to accomplish that dream. Be detailed about what it will take and what you plan to do.

COMMITMENT

Commitment is the day-to-day decision to carry-out the plan of attack. The highest levels of success in any endeavor are brought about by consistency and persistence. People who are truly committed are highly motivated by their dreams. The motivation comes from within and they need little external reinforcement to make things happen. On my office wall, I have a quote from the *Book of Mormon* that has been an inspiration to me for many years. The quote reads, "By small and simple things are great things brought to pass" (Alma 37:6). It is critical to understand this principle when attempting to accomplish something challenging.

Two common emotions high-achieving people experience are anxiety and discouragement. For many people, anxiety is experienced by focusing their thoughts on the future. They worry about things they cannot control and also about their lack of progress toward their goals. When they fail to see the progress they were expecting to make, they become discouraged. I like to compare the pursuit of challenging goals to climbing a steep, muddy mountain. Before scaling the mountain it is normal to stand at the bottom and look up to the summit. That can cause anxiety if a you dwell on the challenging task you are about to begin. Instead, it is best to look up, take a deep breath, and start climbing. There are days you make great progress and can look back down the mountain and feel good about your success. There are also days when you may slip on the muddy slope and slide back down the mountain and actually lose ground. Other days you may put forth tremendous effort and make very little progress because you are just spinning your wheels in the slick mud. However, those who eventually reach the summit get there by continuing to climb, one step in front of the other, until they scale the summit. Anxiety and discouragement are normal emotions for any climber, but those who make it to the top find a way to stay determined, keep motivating themselves, and stay committed to the task at hand.

Jim Loehr, author of *The New Toughness Training for Sports*[3], introduces a concept I believe helps people sustain their motivation level as they pursue their goals. He calls it the "just for today" spirit. It is often difficult to commit to a challenging goal because it can initially seem overwhelming, but most people can do something difficult "just for today." The beauty of this concept is once a person has one successful day it becomes easier to commit to the plan the following day. A basic scientific principle teaches that it takes more energy to get a stationary object moving than it does to keep it moving once it is in motion. This is the principle of momentum. My experience has taught me this principle also applies to scholastic and athletic achievement.

Make a decision to improve something in your life. Plan it out. Visualize yourself doing it well. Tell a friend what you are going to do. Commit yourself to do it "just for today." Remind yourself you do not have to do it forever. You are simply conducting an experiment to do it "just for today." It could be anything including eating a more healthy diet, watching less television, communicating more openly with teammates and coaches, studying more diligently, or exerting more effort in practice. It does not matter. Just choose something that is currently getting in the way of your success and commit yourself to do something about it "just for today." Then, discipline yourself for the day and make it happen. I believe you will discover the following statement to be a truth. George Lorimer said, "You've got to get up each morning with determination if you are going to go to bed with satisfaction." The satisfaction you experience will then be a springboard into the next day. You will begin to gain momentum, and with each passing day, it will get easier and easier to do the thing that once was a stumbling block for you. Thus, successful experiences will not only build your confidence, but also strengthen your commitment and enhance your motivation.

Ashley Lelie, the No. 1 draft pick for the Denver Broncos in 2002, described his transition into professional football as follows. He said, "After you get into practice, you see they're just players, too, just regular people out there giving their all. So, I'm going to try to just imitate them." I have witnessed the same thing happen with many successful college student-athletes. They arrive at college with some uncertainty, having some feeling of intimidation, and then learn their teammates and competitors are just regular people who are extremely committed to what they are doing. They

learn by watching those who succeed at this level and begin to imitate them. At first, many say "I don't know if I can be that committed or work that hard, but if they can do it, I can do it." These types of messages, "just for today," and "if they can do it, I can do it," help athletes get motivated and committed. Committed athletes will experience success, which leads to positive momentum. Once this pattern is firmly established it becomes self-perpetuating.

journal exercise 6

What does it mean to you to be committed? What gets in your way of being as committed as you would like to be? Identify one thing you could do "just for today" to strengthen your commitment level. Do it for one day and write about your experience.

WORK ETHIC

Commitment is the conscious decision to follow a specific course of action that will lead to success. It takes place mentally. Work ethic is the observable actions or behaviors of a committed person or team. For example, I have heard many athletes talk about what is important to them and what they want to accomplish. They may even convince me they are highly motivated and committed to accomplishing great things. However, as I observe their daily behaviors I can generally tell if they are going to accomplish greatness. I have worked with a number of teams who have had ambitious goals such as winning nationals, making it to the final four, going undefeated in conference play, etc. Those who actually succeeded or came close to reaching those types of goals had a different work ethic from those who fell short. You must back up your talk through your actions.

In recent years, I have watched the Men's Volleyball and Women's Cross Country teams win national championships at BYU. I have watched them in the weight room and at practice. Their workouts are intense, focused, and consistent. The coaches and athletes on these teams know what it takes to be successful. They have experienced the highest levels of success because of their work ethic and want to experience the thrill of victory again. They realize it may not always be fun to work hard, but they also know that to experience the most enjoyable moments, such as winning championships, they must regularly outwork their competitors. Teams like this are special because the team norm is to push yourself to the limit. Teammates are united and try to workout together as much as possible. The players buy into their coaches' plan of attack and seldom seek the easy way out. The superstars on these teams do a good job of teaching the rest of the team how to work and no one wants to be the weak link on the team.

In contrast, some of the other teams I have worked with that set equally high goals, but fell short, have had a poor work ethic. I do not question their desire for greatness or even their motivation. Some individuals and teams just do not know what it really takes to achieve the highest levels of success. In other cases, not everyone on the team is willing to pay his or her dues to earn success and, therefore, holds the rest of the team back. In the worst case scenario, the team leaders themselves have been poor examples of what it means to work hard, and the rest of the team followed their lead. One coach challenged his team during a meeting in which summer workout plans were discussed. He said to the team, "You say you want to be a great team and have a great season next year, but from what I've just heard you're headed toward another mediocre year."

Recently, I had an opportunity to talk with Olympic gold medalist Marion Jones. I asked her what the keys to her success have been. She was gracious enough to answer my question and told me a large part of her success can be attributed to her work ethic. Marion said, "I have to be at my best and I can't afford to let anyone else in the world outwork me." Obviously, she cannot keep track of what her competitors are doing around the world. However, Marion needed to believe she was outworking her competitors. That is what drives her to work each day with great intensity. Marion reported that at the end of each workout she asked herself, "Marion, have you honestly put in your best effort today?" She told me there has only been one time when she had to say "no" to that question. Marion's coach overheard the two of us talking and told me a story that impressed me. He

photo courtesy of Vector Sports Management

said one day Marion had finished her workout and was driving home. While driving, she called him concerned because she had forgotten to do part of her workout. He confirmed they missed that particular drill and she returned to the practice facility, dressed out, warmed-up, completed the drill and went home. He said, "That is the kind of athlete she is!"

Before finishing this section, I want to make one comment on overtraining. I have witnessed a small number of athletes become obsessive with their workouts and overtrain. There is a fine line between a work ethic that leads to greatness and overtraining. It is important for athletes to work closely with their coaches and trainers when as they pursue their goals and to be aware of some symptoms of overtraining. Some warning signs include increased resting heart rate, chronic muscle soreness and fatigue, sleep disturbance, changes in appetite, regular sickness, exhaustion, and depression. Overtrained athletes will often complain of being burned out, exhausted, and no longer having fun. The quality of their performances also begin to suffer, and they are slow to recover after a period of rest. It is important to catch these signs early and take time off to recover. Without proper rest, overtrained athletes can suffer serious physical and emotional problems and be forced to miss significant opportunities to participate in the sport they love.

journal exercise 7

Identify someone whose work ethic you admire. What is it about his or her work ethic that impresses you? How would you describe your work ethic? How might you improve it?

SACRIFICE

Nothing of significance is ever accomplished without sacrifice. What are you willing to give up now, to get what you want most–later? M. Scott Peck, author of *The Road Less Traveled*,[4] calls this "delayed gratification." It is human nature to seek to fulfill our needs and desires immediately. When we are hungry, we eat; tired, we sleep; or bored, we seek stimulation. However, disciplined people will think before they act and make decisions now that will pay-off later. For instance, the average person may not jump out of bed on Monday morning thrilled to get to work. In fact, it is common for people to initially struggle to get up and get going. The thought process goes something like this: "The weekend is over already? I can't believe it! I'm not ready to go back to work...but I need to get up and get going. People are counting on me and I really do enjoy my job."

It is vital you realize you always have choices. You are not a slave to your needs, desires, and others' expectations for you. Once you have identified your dream and developed your plan of attack, you then have something to guide your day-to-day decisions. You can routinely ask yourself, "Is this behavior going to help or hinder me from accomplishing my dreams?" Disciplined people regularly choose to sacrifice what they want now for what they want most. As they do so, they often report it is not a sacrifice but just part of what it takes to excel. I vividly remember visiting with an Olympic gymnast about his workout schedule. When I commented about the many sacrifices he was making to pursue his dreams, he said, "It's not a sacrifice; I love what I do."

Another athlete had a different perspective as she looked back on her career. She decided to walk away from an opportunity to play her sport professionally. She had a very bright future, but decided that she was ready to live a more "normal life." She said, "I've given up prom, dating, going to movies with friends, eating foods I like, and living like a normal college student to pursue my athletic career. I'm tired of being sore, fatigued, and having my life so structured." She finished by saying she had a great experience as an athlete and would do it all again if she had the chance, but she was ready to move on to other interests and desires. This athlete was ready to give up sacrificing so much for the sport she loved. Serious athletes make serious sacrifices. Those sacrifices are an indicator of their level of commitment.

A favorite book of mine is called, *Winning isn't Normal*.[5] The author, Keith Bell, writes, "Winning isn't normal...every race has only one winner...that makes winning highly unusual. As such, it requires unusual action...you must do extraordinary things. You can't just be one of the crowd...you have to be willing to stand out and act differently. You can't train, talk, or think like everyone else...you need to consistently take exceptional action." Winners live differently than those they compete against. Not in major ways, but consistently across time they prepare themselves better. The accumulation of sacrifices add up over time to help create the difference between the winners and their competitors. What are you willing to sacrifice for your dreams to come true?

journal exercise **8**

What sacrifices do you currently make as you pursue excellence in your sport? Are there other sacrifices you may need to make, but have not done so yet? If so, what are they?

DISCIPLINED LIFESTYLE

Living a disciplined lifestyle goes hand-in-hand with the principle of sacrifice. Sacrifice entails giving up something to get something better in return. In contrast, discipline is consistently doing those things that are necessary for success. Sacrifice can be summed up by asking, "What do I need to stop doing to improve my chances for success?" Discipline can be determined by asking, "What do I need to keep doing to be the type of person I want to be?" Both sacrifice and discipline are necessary to reach the highest levels of success. For serious athletes, living a disciplined lifestyle is just a way of life. They know discipline will enhance their athletic performance and improve the overall quality of their life. When the athletic career ends, some of the sacrifices that were made will no longer be necessary, but the disciplined lifestyle continues and leads to success in other pursuits. Discipline is required in all of the following areas in order for athletes to maximize their chances for success: physical, mental, relational, and spiritual.

Physical fitness is a pre-requisite to success for any serious student-athlete. There are stories of some athletes, like Babe Ruth, who did not take very good care of themselves physically. However, examples like this are certainly the exception rather than the rule. I also argue, if Babe Ruth was that great while living undisciplined, how much better might he have been had he paid more attention to his physical conditioning? Physical discipline includes proper nutrition, hydration, strength and conditioning, and treatments with the athletic trainer. Familiarize yourself with the latest information through personal study and good networking. Sport nutritionists, strength and conditioning coaches, and athletic trainers can all be excellent resources to help you reach your potential. Be teachable! The best athletes are very well educated about what they need to do to be their best physically and then discipline themselves in such a way that they peak at the proper times. To be the best you must pay careful attention to this critical area of performance.

Serious athletes are also students of their own game. Each sport requires certain technical and strategic expertise. Those who achieve at the highest levels are mentally competent. They have learned through their experiences what works well and what does not. However, personal experience is often not enough. Good coaching is required. Tiger Woods, arguably the best golfer of all time, spent many hours working with his swing coach, Butch Harmon. Good coaches see things the athlete does not. It is impossible for the participant of the sport to objectively analyze all aspects of his or her game. Sometimes major changes are needed, but most of the time adjustments are minor. Most successful athletes give credit for their success to coaches who have mentored and believed in them.

I witnessed one of the best examples of a quality coach-athlete relationship while attending a sport psychology conference in Banff, Canada. Olympic gold medalist Dan O'Brien and his track coach, Rick Sloan, talked about their working relationship. Dan O'Brien may have won the gold medal, but his success was a team approach. His knowledge about what it would take to win the decathlon was shaped by his coach Rick Sloan.

Become a student of your sport. Read about it, learn from your teammates, consult with experts in your sport, and most of all play for a coach you can trust and who can mentor you as a player. Learn to effectively communicate with your coach and be teachable.

Another key to living a disciplined lifestyle is to develop good interpersonal skills. We live in a world that requires us to deal well with other people. Athletes need to be able to interact and communicate well with coaches, trainers, teachers, teammates and fans. You can be an exceptional athlete and fall well short of your potential if you are not coachable. Fans are becoming less tolerant of superstar athletes who are self-centered and unapproachable. Like it or not, athletes do have a social responsibility. Where much is given, much is required. I remember an experience I had as a young child. I went to the high school basketball game in our community. Our team lost a close game to our biggest rival. After the game, my family went to the local pizza restaurant where I happened to see one of the star players in the restroom. It was just he and I, and I was dressed in the team colors. What happened next will always stay with me. He said, "That was a tough game! They outplayed us tonight, but we'll get them next time." He then slapped me five and left the room. He did not need to acknowledge me or talk to me, but he did so in a sportsman-like way that made an impact on

me. "By small and simple things are great things brought to pass."

One of the keys to successful relationships is good communication. I have seen many problems that could have been avoided by better communication. Athletes need to learn to be "thick-skinned" and not take things too personally. The athletic arena is emotionally charged and coaches often give feedback that is brief, direct, and loud. At other times, they make decisions that impact playing time without giving clear explanations why they are doing so. These types of communication, or lack of communication, can lead to misunderstandings that can damage the coach-athlete relationship and lead to hurt feelings.

My counsel to student-athletes in these types of situations is to be proactive. If your coach does something to upset you, talk to him or her. Describe what is bothering you, how you feel about it, and ask for what you need. This is the first step to resolving the problem. Now you can talk things out. This approach is much better than harboring ill feelings toward your coach or playing guessing games about what your coach is thinking. When in doubt, talk it out. In most cases, consistent communication with your coach will help you establish a good working relationship that will enhance your performance. Obviously, timing is critical. During a game is not the right time to discuss playing time concerns, nor is it wise to challenge your coach's decisions in front of other players. However, one-on-one visits can do wonders for the relationship, most of the time.

One final note on relationships. It is difficult to focus on competing well when you are having relationship problems with a significant other in your life such as a spouse, parent, coach, teammate, or friend. One of the best habits you can develop is to work problems out as they arise, before they become burdens you carry around with you. There is no perfect formula. It is simply a matter of talking things out. This may require you to humble yourself and ask for forgiveness or for you to confront the other person on something they are doing to upset you. Good communication requires you to take risks by sharing your emotions with others, but there is nothing more freeing than getting along well with those who are personally involved in your life.

Another important part of a disciplined lifestyle is spirituality. Athletes may differ in their religious beliefs, but I believe there are some fundamental beliefs that most religions teach that are an important part of living successfully. First, there needs to be a healthy balance of having confidence in yourself and living graciously. Numerous coaches and religious leaders encourage people to have an attitude of gratitude for the talents and opportunities with which they have been blessed. Gifted athletes are no more important than anyone else and to treat people poorly because of your athletic status is a mistake. I have seen far too many athletes act as if the red carpet should be rolled out for them 24 hours a day, 7 days a week. Living graciously means being courteous and polite to all people. Furthermore, gracious people live responsibly and do not expect special treatment because they happen to play a game well. Too many student-athletes expect

to be given special treatment in the classroom. This is not only unfair to the other students in the class but also undermines the educational system and enables irresponsibility on the part of the student-athlete.

A second part of spirituality is closely tied to the first. It is living by the golden rule, which is to treat other people like you would like to be treated. Athletics is an entertainment industry. People pay good money to watch a quality performance. The best way to promote this industry is for athletes to have a relationship with their fans. Obviously, during the games the athlete needs to focus on his or her performance, but outside of the competitive arena there are numerous ways to connect with the fans. Signing autographs, getting involved in community service programs, talking with children, and just being friendly and neighborly are just a few ideas.

Spirituality is also impacted by how you live your life. One of the best ways to have peace of mind is to live true to your value-system. I believe every person has a general idea of what is right and what is wrong. I realize there are some gray areas where there are differences of opinion, but most decisions are black and white. Anytime you purposely behave in ways that violate your beliefs or cause harm to others there is an emotional consequence. Emotions such as guilt, shame, discouragement, and depression drain people of positive energy and become a source of distraction. In essence, every wrong choice sidetracks people from their goals and hinders performance. Nobody is perfect. We all make mistakes and can get back on track by once again choosing to live true to our values. Thus, by having a gracious attitude, treating people kindly, and living congruently with our value-system we experience a spirituality that not only leads to happiness but also enhances our performance.

journal exercise

Pick one of the areas of discipline discussed in this section. Write about how your discipline may be lacking in that area and your plans to make improvements.

SUMMARY

Figure 1 is a summary of the building blocks for success. There are two main building blocks for success. Dream big and believe in yourself. These lay the foundation for everything else. Without one or the other, your pursuit of excellence will be limited.

Once your vision is clear and your confidence is high it is critical to have a plan of attack. You must be able to chart your course toward your dreams. To successfully execute this plan, commitment is crucial. A student-athlete's level of commitment can be measured by the intensity of his or her work ethic and the sacrifices he or she is willing to make. The commitment

BUILDING BLOCKS
FOR SUCCESS

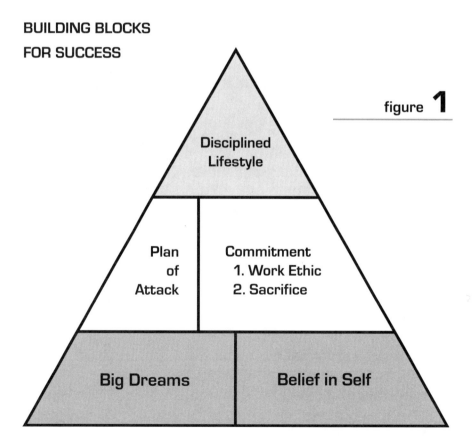

figure **1**

provides the internal motivation to work hard and the willingness to give up something now for something you want most.

Finally, all of the hard-work and sacrifice can be quickly undone if you are not living a disciplined lifestyle. Athletes need to know themselves and what it takes to achieve excellence. They then must discipline their lives physically, mentally, interpersonally, and spiritually. By doing so, they will enjoy the fruits of their labors and experience the success that was once only a dream.

chapter **3**

readiness to play:
the big three

"Everybody has the will to win,
but few have the will to
prepare to win."
– Bobby Knight

I love to learn! It is very important to me to be competent as a sport psychologist and provide quality service. In an attempt to be as knowledgeable as I can, I regularly read books on sport psychology and mental training for performance. In addition, I attend many workshops and seminars to hear the top professionals in the field report on their research and professional experiences. I have learned a tremendous amount from numerous people who are well qualified in the field. I am also indebted to the student-athletes and coaches who have allowed me to share in their world of high-level athletic performance. They have taught me what works and what does not as they prepare to compete. After several years of experience, working everyday in collegiate athletics, I am ready to share what I have learned about what it takes to be ready to play.

The ideas I will share are not uniquely mine. I consider them to be an integrated summary of performance enhancement ideas gathered from the field of sport psychology. The presentation of the information is my best attempt to simplify a large amount of knowledge and present it in a straight-forward approach athletes can use as they seek to prepare themselves to compete. My goal is to present useful information that serious athletes can use as a checklist prior to their performances and as an evaluation tool following each competition. Athletes must know themselves and what works for them. In this chapter, I will present three keys to readiness: activation, emotion, and focus. Then in chapter four, I will describe some practical mental training strategies that athletes can use to adjust their readiness prior to and during performance. Thus, if athletes know what it means to be ready, and then, how to control their readiness, they can take charge of their mental preparation and improve the likelihood of success each time they practice and compete.

ACTIVATION

Activation is the level of physical energy and mental alertness needed to complete a given task. Different activities require different energy levels. For instance, it is very tempting to come home after work and turn on the television because it requires little effort and energy to be a couch potato. On the other hand, many athletes seek to have high activation levels just prior to a challenging workout. They know that without a certain amount of energy it is impossible to complete such tasks. Everybody has fluctuations in their activation levels throughout a typical day. My activation level starts off low early in the morning. To compensate, I like to workout in the morning before I begin the day. My exercise program helps me feel energized physically and alert mentally. I generally feel this way until mid-afternoon. After lunch my energy level takes a dip, unless I am involved in an activity that requires physical exertion or an intense focus. By early evening, my energy level begins to rise until about 10:30 p.m. Then it drops rapidly until I go to sleep. This pattern is pretty consistent if I keep my eating and sleeping schedules regular and workout daily.

Everyone has their own activation patterns. These patterns are connected to the body's circadian rhythms and are pretty consistent, especially if people stick to a regular routine in their daily lives. That is why people sometimes struggle with energy levels while traveling. They may suffer from jet lag but they are also affected by changes in their daily routines. Good coaches know this and seek to prepare their teams by having them change their routines to match the schedule they will adhere to during their upcoming competitions. If they have a game in a different time zone, they have their players adjust their sleep schedules, meal times, and practice hours the week leading up to the performance. By doing so, they hope to have their players in the optimal activation level at game-time.

Think for a moment about your best athletic performances. How would you describe your activation level prior to and during those performances? It is widely accepted in the field of sport psychology that a moderate level of activation, generally, leads to better performances. Simply put, too much or too little activation negatively impacts performance. However, it is more complicated than that for most athletes. Different sports require different

activation levels for success and there are individual differences within the same sport. The key is for you to know what activation level works best for you.

Typical signs that help athletes know they are activated prior to performance include butterflies in the stomach, increased heart and respiration rates, shakiness, muscle tension, increased perspiration, and frequent need to urinate. Most athletes realize these physical symptoms are a normal part of competition. The body's fight or flight system is geared up to meet the perceived challenge awaiting the athlete. The athlete's perception of the upcoming event largely determines the degree to which the body becomes activated. I remember a high school basketball game I participated in against a team we had beaten by 50 points earlier in the season. The other team was terrible! They were young, not very well coached, and their skill level was poor. I remember prior to that game wishing we did not have to play them. I loved to play basketball, but because the game would not be challenging I found it impossible to get up for the game. I was yawning, tired, and sluggish in the moments leading up to the game. I was flat and unemotional. As a result, that game happened to be one of the worst performances of my high school career. In fact, my coach pulled me out of the game in the second quarter and never put me back in the game because I was playing so poorly. This was a textbook case of how under-activation impairs performance.

A few years later, I had the opportunity to play college basketball. On one particular occasion, we played the eventual national champions on our home-court. They were an outstanding team. They were big and athletic, played well as a team, and were well coached. In contrast, we were young, less athletic, and had a mediocre team at best. We knew we had a tremendous challenge ahead of us as we prepared to play them. I was particularly anxious and worried about the possibility of getting embarrassed in front of our home fans. As a result, I played tight, as did the rest of the team. They built a commanding lead within the first few minutes of the game. From that point on, we relaxed and played a solid game against a good team, but we could never recover from our slow start. Our over-activation at the start of the game killed us. I learned a valuable lesson about the importance of

ZONE OF OPTIMAL FUNCTIONING

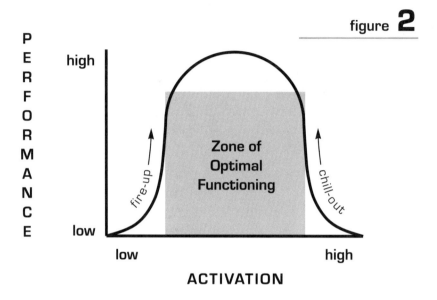

figure **2**

believing in yourself and that you can compete with anybody on a given day if you are ready to play. These two examples illustrate what can happen when an athlete is under- or over-activated.

Yuri Hanin developed a concept known as the Zone of Optimal Functioning (ZOF) in his book *Emotion in Sport.*[6] The theory basically states that there is a moderate level of activation that leads to best performance. As illustrated in Figure 2 above, the Zone of Optimal Functioning is a range of points on the performance curve. There is not an exact amount of activation needed for peak performances. However, there is a point where too much or too little activation leads to performance problems. You need to know what level of activation works best for you. Once you know yourself, you can check-in before performances to determine if you are ready. If not, you can take control and make the adjustments to either chill-out or fire-up. The strategies used to make activation adjustments will be discussed in the next chapter.

I recently traveled with the BYU track team to the NCAA outdoor nationals meet. One morning, I received a phone call from a runner who was scheduled to run later that night. She was concerned her activation level was too high, especially since she would not be racing for several more hours. I had talked to this runner on several other occasions and she found it helpful to talk through her concerns. For her, talking helped release nervous energy. I listened to her and then we discussed a plan of attack for the day that would allow her to get in the right activation level at race time. She called it getting into her "race mode." She decided to relax and take a nap in order to conserve energy for the race. Furthermore, she planned to spend time with other runners on the team so she could keep her mind occupied until she was ready to begin her preparation for "race mode." Then a couple hours before the race she liked to take a shower and do her hair while listening to some music that uplifted her. She timed it so that she would get to the track with only her physical warm-up routine left. If she began to get overly activated she had a strategy that included prayer, deep breathing, positive self-talk, and visualization. This runner knew what activation level worked for her and how to achieve it. I was simply a sounding board for her to remind herself that she was in control and could manage her energy levels through the day so she would be peaking at the appropriate time. In summary, know yourself well enough so you can evaluate your activation level prior to your performances and make adjustments that will move you into your Zone of Optimal Functioning.

journal exercise 10

Reflect on some of your best performances. How did you feel physically prior to and during the performance? Describe your Zone of Optimal Functioning and what you do to get in that state.

EMOTION

Face it, how you feel emotionally does effect how you perform. To some athletes, coaches, and sport scientists this whole topic may seem too "touchy-feely" to take seriously, but I am convinced that emotion matters. Athletes need to know themselves well enough to know how they like to feel at performance time and how they can create that emotional state. In addition, they also need to be aware of feelings that tend to impair their performance. To a large extent athletes can take control of their feelings and thus set the stage for success. I have often witnessed coaches asking their players, "How do you feel?" in the moments leading up to competition. I think this is a valuable question to ask. It gives athletes an opportunity to check-in and make adjustments if necessary.

I have asked many athletes over the years what emotions are present when they are at their best athletically. The answers vary from person to person, but there are some key emotions most athletes identify. These emotions can be categorized into some common themes. With few exceptions, athletes identify confidence as a critical emotion for success. Confidence is the feeling of being ready and capable of meeting the challenge that lies ahead. The self-talk of a confident person is: "I'm ready to compete and I will be successful." Trust is the attitude of the confident athlete. I talked with a confident golfer just prior to her team's regional meet and she told me the following, "I've done everything I can to prepare myself, I have a good plan for the day, and I'll make whatever adjustments I need throughout the round." This is a great example of a trusting attitude that feeds into an athlete's feeling of confidence. Trusting athletes seem to understand the importance of "surrendering to the moment" just prior to performance. At that point, there is nothing else you can do to prepare except relax and let it happen.

Another key emotion is optimism. Optimists go into a performance with positive expectations. They see competition as an opportunity to excel and visualize themselves being successful before they even enter the athletic arena. Positive expectancy is critical for success. There are differences along the same continuum, as illustrated below in figure 3. At one end, you have an athlete that "doubts" him or herself, in the middle is the athlete who "hopes" to do well, and at the other end is the athlete who "expects" to do well. The feeling of optimism is created by these positive expectations.

figure **3**

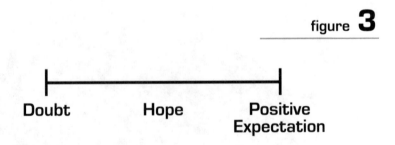

Most athletes also correlate enjoyment with good performance. When they are at their best they are generally excited, enthusiastic, and having fun. When athletes enjoy themselves they are free to simply play the sport they love without unnecessary expectations and pressures. This freedom allows them to have a calm mind and a relaxed body. The conditions under which peak performances generally occur.

Determination or competitiveness are other emotions that athletes often identify as critical to successful performance. Other descriptors of these emotions include resiliency, mental toughness, and persistence. Determination is the feeling that allows athletes to meet the demands of a challenging situation. Competitive athletes stay motivated to keep going when others typically throw in the towel and quit. They also tend to bounce back quicker from adversity. I am reminded of the mental battle experienced by many endurance-sport athletes. Even when they are fully prepared to compete, they experience a certain degree of fear and anxiety because they know they are about to put their body through a painful experience. However, this anxiety is countered by the way these athletes talk themselves into approaching their fears and worries and conquering the challenge awaiting them. Ultimately, determined athletes are better able to motivate themselves and as a result their training is more thorough. Their competitive fire is also more intense.

A healthy dose of anticipatory anxiety also seems to lead to good performance. Most athletes do experience some realistic and rational worries about their upcoming performances. It is normal to wonder if you are really capable of meeting the challenge that lies ahead of you. The key to dealing with anticipatory anxiety is to recognize it, normalize it, and then refocus on the game plan. As long as you focus on controlling the things you do have control over, and choose not to worry about those things you cannot control, you can effectively manage this emotion. This emotion is very closely connected to an athlete's activation level. Strategies used to manage activation levels will also help relieve anticipatory anxiety and vise versa.

Some final emotions that are often discussed seem to have a spiritual dimension to them. These include the feelings of being centered, at peace, and having gratitude for the opportunity to perform as well as feeling connected to teammates, coaches, and the performance environment. Like most feelings, it is hard to put into words what this really feels like. Some describe it as a sense of harmony or oneness with themselves and the game they play. When they experience this feeling they describe an effortlessness to their performance and sometimes a distortion in time. One runner recently described her race at nationals where she peaked as a runner. She said, "I just felt so smooth, and the race seemed so easy, and before I knew it the race was about over and I could not believe how good I felt and how quickly time passed."

In summary, the key emotions most athletes describe include confidence, optimism, enjoyment, determination, competitiveness, anticipatory anxiety, and a combination of emotions such as peace, connectedness, gratitude, and being centered. It is not my intention to provide an exhaustive list of feelings every athlete must have in order to be successful. Every athlete is different, every competition is unique, and what worked for you last year may change some next year. However, I do believe these emotions are important to consider as you discover what works best for you. Again, the key is for you to know yourself well enough so you can take charge and create the emotional state that will give you the highest probability for successful performance.

Before I conclude this section, I would like to identify and briefly describe some feelings that have a tendency to impair athletic performance. One of the major emotions that gets in the way of good performance is fear. Many athletes struggle with the fear of failure. They are afraid of rejection from others, of letting themselves down, and having to face the possibility they are not as good as they thought they were in the sport they love. Others are afraid of injury, embarrassment, and the raised expectations that come with success. Regardless of what athletes fear, this emotion will lead to poor performance if it is not managed well. When athletes are at their best they are decisive, aggressive, and willing to take risks. However, fear causes athletes to be tentative, cautious, and play it safe. Research in psychology clearly shows the best way to overcome fear is exposure. You must change your self-talk, face the fear head-on, and be willing to take the risk that something bad might happen. As you do so, the fear generally loses its power over you and you will likely discover the fear you experienced was an exaggerated emotional reaction to a situation that was not really that scary.

Excessive worry is another emotion that can negatively impact performance. Worry is fed by "what if" thinking. "What if I false start," "What if I fumble the ball," "What if I get in the game and miss my first shot,"

"What if the weather is bad," "What if my competitors are better trained than me." Every athlete has a choice about what they want to think about. By choosing to focus on things that could go wrong, and things out of your control, you are choosing to worry. If you catch yourself worrying more than you would like, simply distract yourself by focusing your attention on something else or choose to think about positive possibilities and focus on imagining yourself having success.

Another performance-inhibiting emotion is uncontrolled anger. This emotion seldom leads to anything positive. For some people frustration and anger can lead to a determined response. Their motivation to face challenges may be enhanced and the energy necessary to carry out difficult tasks is increased. There is, however, a difference between anger that is channeled in productive ways and anger that destroys. When athletes allow their anger to get out of control, they lose their focus and engage in behaviors that impair their performance and can cause harm to themselves and others. For athletes who struggle with uncontrolled angry outbursts, having a well thought-out coping plan can be helpful in managing future occurrences of frustration. A coping plan includes being more aware of what pushes your buttons and how you will choose to respond differently in the future. Go back to previous situations in which you lost control and re-write the ending to how you responded then. The plan might include taking a deep breath, telling yourself "I'm in control," walking away for a few seconds to regain your composure, getting a drink to cool off, or even smiling and having a sense of humor. The point is to have something you can do quickly that will manage your anger so you can use it productively to enhance your performance.

Prolonged discouragement is another emotion that is seldom helpful to athletes. This feeling has a tendency to drain your energy and lead to other counterproductive emotions such as self-doubt, hopelessness, pessimism, and even depression. Obviously, if you compete in athletics long enough you will experience some discouragement. It is as much a part of sports as any other emotion. In fact, athletes who have experienced bouts of discouragement are better able to savor the thrill of victory when it comes. Discouragement comes from having unmet expectations, coaching decisions that seem unfair, losing, injury, and unexpected changes. So, it is not the emotion of discouragement that is the problem. It is getting stuck in discouragement and allowing it to be more extreme than it needs to be. I still remember losing in the district basketball tournament my junior year in high school. I had put my whole heart and soul into getting to the state tournament. When we lost, one game before making it to the state playoffs, I experienced a number of emotions for the next few months, including numbness, shock, discouragement, and depression. Looking back, my reaction was excessive and unhealthy, but I did learn how to better handle loss from that experience. At some point, you have to tell yourself, "get over it, it is time to move on," and then reconnect with life by setting new goals and focusing your attention on the present instead of the past. It is easier said than done, but it is critical for your future success.

Thus, fear, worry, anger, and discouragement are all part of the human experience. Most athletes will experience these emotions to some degree. I believe they all have a purpose and a function, but when taken to extremes these emotions can and will negatively impact performance. Again, the key is to know how these emotions affect you, and have a strategy to best deal with them so you are in control and ready to play in the future.

journal exercise **11**

Describe the emotional state present when you perform your best. How do you create it? What emotions interfere with your performance? How have you learned to best deal with those feelings?

FOCUS

Athletes are often told by coaches to "concentrate" or "focus," but are seldom told what that really means or how to do it. Concentration is a process of focusing on cues or stimuli that are directly relevant for the successful performance of a task. In any given performance, there are an abundance of internal and external stimuli that can capture an athlete's attention. Internal stimuli include both thoughts and feelings athletes experience prior to and during a performance. External stimuli include anything taking place in the performance environment. Successful performers learn to selectively attend to those cues that enhance performance and by doing so avoid focusing on irrelevant cues that distract them and lead to poor performance.

Concentration also requires a here-and-now mentality. Successful performers live in the present. They do not worry about yesterday's loss or tomorrow's game while they are competing. Likewise, their mistakes or successes earlier in the competition do not carry over into what they are doing now. During competition, they take each possession, point, race, or stroke one at a time since that is the only time they have any control over. The past is gone and the future is in the distance. Thus, concentration cannot be forced and does not require hard work. It is a passive process of being totally absorbed in the present and in tune with your competitive environment and the appropriate cues.

Robert Nideffer is one of the leading experts in the field of sport psychology in the area of attention control training. In his book, *Athlete's Guide to Mental Training*,[7] he describes two different dimensions of concentration.

The first is the width of attentional focus or the amount of information you are trying to focus on at a given time. The width can vary from narrow to broad.

The second dimension is the direction of the focus. Athletes focus their attention externally or internally. When put together these two dimensions make four attentional quadrants as seen in Figure 4.

DIMENSIONS OF CONCENTRATION

figure **4**

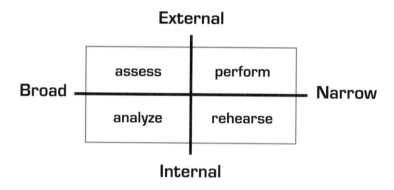

To illustrate each dimension of attention I will use an example of a golfer hitting a shot from the fairway. Imagine the golfer walking up to her ball before she hits her second shot. As she approaches her ball she assesses the situation. Her focus is broad and external at this point. She looks at how her ball is sitting in the grass, how far it is away from the hole, the pin placement and possible hazards, and checks to see if there is any wind that may effect the shot. Once she has fully assessed the situation, she then takes all of the information she has gathered and begins to analyze what she should do. Her focus is still broad, but her planning takes place internally. After she has put together her strategy, she mentally rehearses what she has planned to do. Her focus at this point remains internal, but she begins to narrow in on the most important cues to successfully execute the shot. The rehearsal is generally composed of visualization or talking her way through the keys to successful execution of this shot. After her rehearsal, she is ready to put her plan into action and perform the shot. Her focus remains narrow, but she shifts her concentration to some simple external cues like "see the ball" or "accelerate through the ball."

Most athletes will go through similar shifts in focus while participating in their sport. Their attention will shift back and forth among the quadrants throughout a practice or competition. In some sports, like running a 100-meter dash, the focus on assessing, analyzing, and rehearsal may all take place during the preparation period prior to running the race. At race time, the performance focus will mainly be narrow-external for the entire duration of the race. This differs from the football quarterback on a pass play. He must call the play in the huddle, and then immediately shift to a broad-external focus as he makes the initial read of the defense. He then takes that information and moves to a broad-internal focus as he decides to go with the called play or call an audible. There is not a lot of time for a rehearsal of the play mentally, but there is a split second plan how the play will unfold. This may even take place unconsciously for an experienced quarterback who has had numerous repetitions in practice or game situations. Finally, the focus moves external and narrow as he calls the snap-count and executes the play.

These shifts in attention vary from sport to sport. In some sports, like golf, they are slow and methodical. In other sports, like a basketball point-guard running a fastbreak, they are split-second changes. It is helpful to think about your sport and understand what the attentional demands are on you as an athlete. Again, much of the assessment, analyzing, and rehearsal will take place prior to competition and will be an integral part of an athlete's performance routine. Good preparation allows athletes to spend most of their time simply executing what they have practiced and rehearsed.

One problem many athletes have experienced is called "paralysis by analysis." Some athletes complicate things at performance time by over analyzing what they are doing. They end up thinking way too much (internal) instead of focusing on a few simple cues (external) that will enhance their performance. This problem can be explained as poor preparation or a lack of trust in the skills they are executing. When athletes are at their best they are well prepared, trusting, and keep their approach as simple as possible. This creates a relaxed body and calm mind, which allows the athlete to shift his or her focus effortlessly through the different dimensions of attention. Again, most of these shifts take place out of the awareness of the

relaxed, trusting athlete. For instance, Tony Gwynn, the great hitter from the San Diego Padres, said when he was at his best as a hitter he had a simple focus: "See the ball, hit the ball." Obviously, he is shifting in and out of the various dimensions of focus each time he is up to bat, but much of that took place with very little, if any, conscious thought. This allowed him to focus most of his attention on simply seeing and hitting the ball.

Another common focusing problem is paying too much attention to uncontrollables, or things outside of the athlete's control. For instance, a basketball player might get a bad call from a referee during a game. From that point on, he may continue to fume over the injustice, and play out of control or too tentative for the rest of the game.

A runner I worked with on the cross country team at BYU found the phrase "control the controllables" to be very helpful for her as she prepared for races. She came in before the major competitions and talked about all of her worries. I generally just listened as she released some of her nervous energy. She would catch herself worrying and say, "I just need to focus on controlling the controllables, huh?" We then talked about what were the controllables. Her anxiety seemed to dissipate and she walked away with a plan that included the basics of eating right, hydrating, getting good rest, developing her race plan with her coach's input, and rehearsing the plan through imagery. That got her ready to perform. Then on race day, her attention shifted from preparation to execution of the race plan. The point I am making is that a lot of stress can be relieved, and focus can be improved, if athletes will simply identify what they can control and focus on that instead of the many things they cannot control. Simple is better when it comes to focusing.

One final note on concentration. It is very difficult to sustain attention on anything for an extended period of time. Most sports have some built in opportunities to unfocus for brief periods of time. I believe it is important for athletes to unfocus from their sport during these periods of time so they can refocus better when it is time to perform again. Even if it is only for a couple of seconds. The best way to unfocus is to focus on something unrelated to your sport briefly. For example, a tennis player might look up in the crowd during a change over and see who might be there supporting her. A golfer might take in the beautiful scenery of the golf course between shots. A basketball player may focus on the opportunity to relax during a substitution break by briefly talking to a teammate on the bench. Most sports have built-in opportunities to focus on something unrelated to the sport for brief periods of time. I think one of the keys to good focus is knowing when and how to focus and unfocus. The natural shifts between these states will enhance the athlete's ability to really lock-in when it is necessary to do so.

journal exercise **12**

What are some of the things that distract you prior to or during performance? When you are performing your best, what cues are you focusing on? Using the quadrants discussed in this section, describe what shifts you make as you perform your sport.

PUTTING IT ALL TOGETHER

In chapter three, I have written about three keys to getting ready to play. Athletes need to get themselves properly activated, in the right emotional state, and focused on the cues that will lead to successful performance. It is also important to understand how an athlete's activation, emotion, and focus interact. For instance, if an athlete comes to practice with a low activation level, his or her emotional state and focus will also be impacted. So, the coach may get upset with the athlete for not paying attention and being apathetic when the problem stems from low activation. The coach may respond by yelling at the athlete and punishing him or her with a set of push-ups or running sprints. All of the sudden, the intensity of practice picks up and the player is more focused and motivated to compete.

What is the explanation for the change? It is a complex question. In reality, the athlete's activation, emotion, and focus have all been affected. The physical exercise raises the activation level by increasing the athlete's heart and respiration rate. You might also expect the athlete to feel irritated at the coach or upset with him or herself for performing so poorly. In either case, the motivation is likely to change and the athlete's focus improves. A change in one area can affect the other two as well. Let me give three examples.

I worked with a golfer who was frustrated because he noticed a pattern in which he would play good golf until the end of each round. He believed it was a matter of becoming unfocused due to fatigue after spending a full day golfing. We tried a few focusing strategies to help him deal with the problem. However, he noticed little improvement and became more discouraged with his problem. Finally, we had him monitor how he felt physically and emotionally at the end of each round. We noticed a pattern of him feeling tired and having low energy. Upon further discussion, it became clear he was likely dehydrated and because he failed to refuel through proper eating, his energy level was low by the end of the round. By making some simple adjustments in his food and liquid intake and having a few mental strategies available to raise his activation level, his focus improved dramatically.

Another example of the interaction between activation, emotion, and focus involved a tennis player. Her coach referred her to see me because she became very angry at times on the court and then her game would fall apart after her anger outbursts. As we examined what led to her "temper tantrums," it became clear the main predictor was her pre-match emotional state. If she came to practice or a match in a "bad mood," the chance of her having an outburst was greatly increased. So, we focused on managing her pre-match emotions and developed a coping strategy she could use when she became upset on the court. The strategy included a combination of self-talk statements such as, "I'm in control," "I'm going to enjoy my match today," and "I can deal with any challenge I face on the court," as well as some deep breathing, and anger management exercises. One exercise was to slow down her pace between points when she became frustrated, by walking back to the fence, drying off her sweat with a towel, and then, while putting down the towel, saying "next point, refocus." She found that when she took control of her emotions before a match she seldom had to use the anger management exercises during the match. This also helped to create the proper activation level, and she maintained better focus throughout the match.

Finally, I have seen a common issue for many college student-athletes. During their competitive season they get spread pretty thin because of the demands of school, travel, daily practice, and games. There just does not seem to be enough hours in the day. During the busiest times of the season, it is common for athletes to come to practice unfocused. It is not because they want to be unfocused at practice, it is more the reality that they have a paper to write that night or a major exam the next morning. As a result of being distracted, their focus suffers. When athletes are trying to focus on too many things at once, their stress levels rise as does their activation. One skill I try to teach athletes is to "be where you are." When it is time to practice have your attention there. Have a natural transition point where you move from being a student to becoming an athlete. For instance, lock all other worries up in your locker after getting dressed for practice and remind yourself they can be dealt with after practice. Then shut the locker and zero in on your sport. When practice is over and it is time to study, leave your worries about your sport in the athletic complex, which will allow you to focus on studying. Have a specific place to study. Each time you enter that environment you have one purpose: to study. Athletes who become skilled at "being where they are" are much more focused and productive. Thus, by developing the skill of focus they gain greater control over their activation levels and emotions.

chapter **4**

mental
training tools

"The winners in life think constantly in
terms of I can, I will, I am. Losers, on the
other hand, concentrate their waking
thoughts on what they should have or
would have done, or what they can't do."

– Dennis Waitley

T o be ready to play, athletes need to be properly activated, in the right emotional state,
and focused on the task at hand. Athletes
must know what works best for them in
each of these three areas. Self-awareness is critical for
consistent, high-level performance. Many athletes with
whom I regularly consult are able to easily identify and
describe their optimal performance states. It becomes
automatic and before each performance they do a quick
check-in with themselves to make sure they are ready to
play. I like to use the analogy of an airline pilot and his
pre-flight checks of the plane. It would be terribly
unwise and dangerous for the pilot to step into the plane
and immediately leave the gate for departure. Instead,
time is taken to carefully make sure all systems are ready
for takeoff. Athletes who are serious about their performances go through a similar process to make sure

they are mentally and physically ready to play.

For example, a pre-game check-in may go something like this: "Okay, how is my activation level? I'm feeling energetic and pumped for the game tonight. However, I am a little too tight and slightly over activated. I need to loosen my muscles and bring my heart rate down a bit. Emotionally, I'm feeling confident, excited, and I'm really enjoying the opportunity to compete. I'm right where I need to be. My main focus tonight will be on playing decisive and aggressive. Keeping things simple and executing the game plan. My three focal points will be...".

Here is an example of a pre-practice check-in. "Man, I'm really flat today. I'm tired and feel like I have no energy. I need to get my activation level up or it is going to be a long day. Emotionally, my confidence has not been very good lately and I am lacking motivation. I also haven't been having any fun. I need to do something to change that today. I'm going to focus on these three goals for the day...". As you can see, the check-in before a game or practice is simple and straightforward. It takes very little time, but can have a dramatic effect on performance.

In this chapter, I will discuss some practical strategies athletes can use to get themselves ready to play. It is one thing to be aware you are not ready to play, but if you do not have some tools or strategies to make necessary changes then your awareness is inconsequential. These tools are designed to be used quickly and in the performance environment. However, these mental training skills will require some consistent practice before they will have their full impact. Serious athletes need to discipline themselves to regularly practice these skills. Athletes who have consistent check-ins and make adjustments using the tools discussed in this chapter will have a mental advantage over many of their competitors at performance time and will be mentally prepared to perform their best.

SELF-TALK

Self-talk is the quiet, and in some cases not so quiet, conversations that you have with yourself prior to, during, and after your performances. Self-statements like "way to go," "you can do it,"or "you can't do anything right" are examples of self-talk during performances. What you tell yourself directly affects how you feel and perform. Positive self-talk enhances your confidence and improves your ability to perform well. Negative self-talk often leads to feelings of doubt, fear, or anxiety, which limit your ability to perform to your true potential. By improving your self-talk, you can stay more focused during practice and competition, motivate yourself to perform better, and experience greater success.

Pretend you are teaching a child how to shoot a basketball. You would demonstrate how, explain the important aspects of this skill, and then encourage her to do her best. If she made the shot, you would reinforce what she did well and give genuine praise. "Way to go Jennie, I liked your follow-through!" If she missed, you would encourage her and give her some brief instructional feedback. "It's okay, bend your knees and focus on your target." This type of teaching comes natural when we keep the right perspective. However, many performers lose the proper perspective when they critique their own performance. When they do well they seldom praise themselves or even minimize their success. They just expect to do well all of the time. Nevertheless, performers tend to be very critical of themselves and their abilities when they do not perform well. Athletes might say, "Finally, why couldn't I have started playing better earlier in the game?" They are impatient, negative, and engage in self-talk that lowers their confidence and their belief that they can succeed. An example of this type of self-talk might be, "You can't do anything right! You don't belong at this level of competition." Imagine talking to a young performer like you talk to yourself. In many cases, you would take the fun out of performing and ruin the youngsters confidence. The obvious conclusion is to use self-talk that teaches, inspires, motivates, and enables you to believe in yourself and have fun. You can be your greatest fan or your worst enemy. You decide; the choice is yours!

Awareness is often the first step to change. You can only change your self-talk when you can identify what it is you are saying to yourself. Next time you perform be aware of your internal dialogue with yourself. After the performance, journal how well you performed, your level of confidence, and what you said to yourself that impacted your performance in a positive or negative way. Think of past performances and try to remember your self-talk. Watch yourself on videotape to help recall your emotions and thought processes. Have your coach or teammates help you monitor your verbalizations during practice or competition. These are all ways to monitor what you say to yourself.

To change your self-talk you simply need to stop your negative thinking as soon as you are aware of it. Tell yourself, "Stop!" Then use a cue word or phrase to help you refocus, such as, "Be positive, you can do it." Take a few deep breaths to clear your mind, and replace your negative self-statement with its positive counterpart. The main point is to stop the negativity, decide to be positive, and then perform with a clear mind. Changing your self-talk requires desire on your part, an awareness of your self-statements, and persistent practice and effort.

One final note. Positive self-talk is more than just stroking your ego and helping you feel happy inside. You are actually programming your mind with each self-statement you make. This programming ultimately impacts how you feel and how you perform. If you tell yourself, "I can never make a pressure putt," or "I never perform well in big games," you program your mind. Next time you are standing over an important putt or preparing for a "big race" you will likely experience feelings of doubt and unnecessary pressure because you already programmed your mind for such an experience. As a result, your performance will suffer. Your feelings and performance become self-fulfilling prophecies of previous self-statements. Now, I am not suggesting one negative self-statement will make you perform poorly. We all make negative self-evaluations occasionally. It is the repetition that causes the biggest problem. The greatest athletes love the pressure situations and participate in athletics for those moments. Their self-talk helps them rise to the occasion and meet most challenges successfully. Why? Because they have programmed themselves for such success through consistent, positive programming. Positive programming improves the probability athletes will have success. Then, when the successes occur, it becomes easier to be positive, which leads to more success. The cycle becomes self-perpetuating.

journal exercise **13**

For the next couple of days, pay attention to your self-talk. Then write about what you discover. If your self-talk tends to be negative, try changing it and observe how this affects your performance.

IMAGERY

Imagery is defined as using all of your senses to create or recreate an experience in your mind. Think of imagery as "practicing in your head," or as "going to the movies of your mind." Imagery is a daydream with a purpose. When used systematically, in conjunction with physical practice and good coaching, it can have amazing results. Leonard Myles-Mills, the two-time NCAA National Champion in the 100-meter dash, identified imagery as an important part of his success in track. He said, "I visualize the race being run and I have won...I see the other athletes trailing behind me and that is exactly what happened when the race is actually run...The similarity between my imagery and the race is scary sometimes...it really increases my confidence."

The mind does not know the difference between what is real and what is vividly imagined. Think for a moment about some of the dreams you have had while sleeping. Dreams can cause a wide range of emotions such as fear, sadness, excitement, and pleasure. Dreams also impact the body's activation system. Think of scary dreams that cause you to wake-up abruptly. These experiences can make the heart pound, body sweat, and muscles tight. Your fight or flight system becomes activated. Physically and emotionally your body is responding to something that is not even real. However, the mind and body treat vivid dreams as real experiences.

This understanding is important for explaining why imagery works. One of the best ways to develop confidence in yourself is to have a successful experience. That is how most athletes become interested in their sports. They try a new sport and experience some success. The success they experience is enjoyable so they keep doing it. The more they do it the better they get. Thus, it is the successful experiences that lead to increases in confidence and competency.

Imagery is so useful because athletes can create successful experiences in their mind at any time and in any place. When imagery skills are well developed, the images are vivid and have a positive impact psychologically. Successful mental experiences become mental blueprints for actual experiences. The power of imagery comes from mental repetition. It is an accepted truth that practice is an essential part of perfecting any skill. When imagery is used in conjunction with physical practice, an athlete can dramatically increase the number of positive repetitions.

Imagery is a skill that must be practiced regularly. With practice, it becomes more vivid and real. I personally recommend using imagery four or five days a week. Each imagery session only needs to last 5 to 10 minutes. Like self-talk, you are programming your mind for success each time you create positive images. Use all of your senses (seeing, hearing, tasting, smelling, moving, and emotion) to enhance imagery vividness. To gain better control of your images, start simple and increase the complexity of your imagery as your skills improve. You can also facilitate imagery through relaxation. A relaxed body and clear mind will enhance the experience. You may want to begin by taking a few deep breaths, closing your eyes, and simply imagining a ball in your hand. What do you see, feel, and smell? Next imagine yourself bouncing the ball. Feel the movement and rhythm. Continue to increase the complexity until you are imagining actual performances.

Use both internal and external perspectives. Internal imagery is from the perspective of the performer. See what the runner sees, feel the pavement under your feet, hear your feet as they hit the ground, taste the sweat in your mouth, etc. External imagery is from the perspective of a spectator. See yourself performing on the movie screen of your mind. The internal perspective may allow you to use more senses, but both perspectives are useful. Find what works best for you.

Image different aspects of your performance. Image perfect performances, positive responses to adversity, times when you exhibit mental toughness, your pre-performance routine and ideal activation level, and winning the competition. Be creative, it is your movie and you write the script. By changing your imagery experience it remains stimulating.

Once you have adequately developed your imagery skills, you can use imagery quickly and efficiently in practice and competition situations. I call these experiences "snapshot" images. These are imagery clips that last from 3-5 seconds and can be used on the go. For example, a tennis player can visualize a strong return just prior to receiving his opponents serve. Snapshot images can also be paired with cue words to enhance their effectiveness, such as "quick feet," "smooth and easy," "attack," and "focus." The images and cue words should be simple, instructional, and positive to be most effective.

Imagery is an activity that takes place mostly in the right hemisphere of the athlete's brain. Research suggests athletes perform best when the right side of the brain is more activated than the left at the time of their performance. By activating the right side of the brain through imagery, the left side automatically becomes less activated. Two problematic left brain activities include analytical thinking and verbal instructions. Simply put, analysis leads to paralysis and over-thinking impairs performance. By focusing on visual and kinesthetic images, athletes are better able to prepare their minds to trust their preparation and focus on the task at hand. Thus, imagery is an important mental skill for athletes to use as they seek to improve skills, rehearse strategy, enhance confidence, and prepare their minds for performance.

journal exercise **14**

Practice imagery for 10 minutes a day for the next five days. Write about your experience and its effect on your performance.

RELAXATION – "CHILL-OUT"

Being able to relax the body and calm the mind is a critical skill for athletes to develop. Relaxation exercises can help athletes to manage stressful times in their lives and can be used to reduce over-activation in performance settings. Most athletes can remember a time when their body was too activated and their mind was racing prior to an important competition. This can be a helpless feeling when you do not have an effective way to deal with the situation. In fact, the activation level of athletes often increases when they realize they are over-activated. They begin to worry that their activation level will negatively effect their performance and this worry leads to even higher levels of activation and the athlete gets caught in a vicious cycle.

The first step in managing over-activation is recognizing your body is too charged up. Typical signs include increases in heart and respiration rates, cold hands and feet, sweating, butterflies in the stomach, shakiness, yawning, increased need to urinate, pacing, and feelings of nervousness, worry, and fear. Once you are aware you need to relax and calm down you can regain control of your mind and body. I generally recommend athletes begin by using a combination of deep breathing and self-talk. Begin by taking three deep breaths. This is a signal to your mind and body that you are going to take control and calm down. Sustained deep breathing causes a physiological change in the body that includes slowing the heart rate, reducing muscle tension, and increasing blood flow to the extremities (hands and feet). These changes are experienced as a "relaxation response."

Changes in self-talk can also help relax the body and calm the mind. Athletes need to remember they are responsible for getting themselves over-activated in the first place. They programmed this response by what they told themselves about the situation they are stressed about. For instance, an athlete might say, "This is a big game, I must perform my absolute best." This type of self-talk leads to the athlete feeling extreme pressure and the body's fight or flight mechanism kicks in as the athlete prepares for battle. However, just as the athlete talked herself into over-activation, she can talk herself into relaxation. She might say something like, "Yes, I would like to do my best today, and I expect to do so because I have prepared well." Another response might be, "Today is going to be fun; I generally perform my best when the competition is challenging." To deal directly with self-produced stress she might say, "Chill-out, you're getting too worked up and you need to bring down your activation level." Each athlete needs to be aware of what types of things he or she typically says that leads to over-activation and which types of calming statements work best to bring about the "relaxation response."

Often times, sitting down, taking three deep breaths, and using calming statements can bring about the desired change in activation level. However, this may not be adequate when an athlete has allowed the activation to get too high. In those cases, additional breathing and muscle relaxation exercises may be needed to bring the activation level down. Below, I have provided the instructions for exercises I regularly use with athletes that are simple and can be used to bring about a relaxation response quickly and effectively. Remember, these exercises need to be practiced regularly if they are going to be useful on game day.

Complete Breathing Exercise

Sit or lie down in a comfortable position. Close your eyes and concentrate on taking complete breaths. Gently place one hand on your stomach, just above your belly button, but below your rib cage. Now focus on making your hand rise and fall as you inhale and exhale. Complete breathing requires you to breath in a manner that allows you to use your full lung capacity. If you are doing this exercise properly, your hand should move up and down with each breath. Now take two or three minutes and focus exclusively on making each breath deep and complete. As you do so, be aware of how your body becomes more and more relaxed and your mind becomes calm and focused.

Natural Breathing Exercise

Sit or lie down in a comfortable position. Close your eyes and concentrate on your natural breathing rhythm. Don't worry about changing it. Just notice how it feels as you inhale and exhale. Maintain your focus on your breathing for a few minutes. If you get distracted in any way, just notice the source of the distraction and then gently bring your focus back to your breathing. As you do so, you will become relaxed and experience a state of peacefulness.

Slow Breathing Exercise

Sit or lie down in a comfortable position. Close your eyes and bring your attention to your breathing. Don't worry about changing it. Just notice how it feels as you inhale and exhale. Now for the next couple of minutes, begin to change your breathing rhythm. Focus on making each breath slower and deeper than the one before until you find a rhythm that is slow, deep, and comfortable. Maintain that rhythm and notice how your breathing leaves you feeling centered and ready for any challenge you might face.

Progressive Muscle Relaxation

Sit or lie down in a comfortable position. Close your eyes, take a couple of deep breaths, and then tighten all the muscles in your face, head, and jaw. Hold the tension for 5 seconds and then release. Notice the difference between the tension and the relaxation... (pause for 5 to 10 seconds with each...)

Again, tighten all the muscles in your face, head, and jaw. Hold the tension for 5 seconds and then release. Enjoy the relaxation you feel in your face, head, and jaw...

Next, tighten all the muscles in your neck, shoulders, and upper back. Hold the tension for 5 seconds and then release. Notice the difference between the tension and the relaxation... Again, tighten all the muscles in you neck, shoulders, and upper back. Hold the tension for 5 seconds and then release. Enjoy the relaxation you feel in your neck, shoulders, and upper back...

Now tighten all the muscles in your hands, forearms, biceps, triceps, and chest. Hold the tension for 5 seconds and then release. Notice the difference between the tension and the relaxation... Again, tighten all the muscles in you hands, forearms, biceps, triceps, and chest. Hold the tension for 5 seconds and then release. Enjoy the relaxation you feel in your

hands, forearms, biceps, triceps, and chest... Now tighten all the muscles in your stomach and lower back. Hold the tension for 5 seconds and then release. Notice the difference between the tension and the relaxation... Again, tighten all the muscles in you stomach and lower back. Hold the tension for 5 seconds and then release. Enjoy the relaxation you feel in your stomach and lower back...

Now tighten all the muscles in your buttocks and thighs. Hold the tension for 5 seconds and then release. Notice the difference between the tension and the relaxation... Again, tighten all the muscles in your buttocks and thighs. Hold the tension for 5 seconds and then release. Enjoy the relaxation you feel in your buttocks and thighs...

Now tighten all the muscles in your calves, ankles, and feet. Hold the tension for 5 seconds and then release. Notice the difference between the tension and the relaxation... Again, tighten all the muscles in you calves, ankles, and feet. Hold the tension for 5 seconds and then release. Enjoy the relaxation you feel in your calves, ankles, and feet...

Now tighten all the muscles throughout your body. Hold the tension for 5 seconds and then release. Notice the difference between the tension and the relaxation... Again, tighten all the muscles throughout your body. Hold the tension for 5 seconds and then release. Enjoy the relaxation you feel throughout your body.

Passive Muscle Relaxation

Sit or lie down in a comfortable position. Close your eyes, take a couple of deep breaths, and focus your attention on the muscles throughout your head, face, and jaw... (pause for 5 to 7 seconds with each...) Allow those muscles to become loose, limp, and comfortable... Feel any remaining tension drain out of that part of your body... Now focus on the muscles in your neck, shoulders, and upper back. Notice those muscles becoming smooth, loose, and comfortable... Just let the tension leave that part of your body... Now allow the tension drain out of your upper arms, forearms, wrists, hands, and fingers... your arms are becoming loose, limp, and relaxed... Now notice the muscles in your stomach and lower back becoming relaxed... Just let any tension or tightness leave that part of your body...

Notice how relaxed your arms, upper body, and head feel at this moment... Now let the tension drain from your buttocks and thighs... Notice those strong muscle becoming loose and limp and comfortable... The tension continues to drain downward past your knees, calves, through your ankles, feet and toes... Notice the relaxed state of your entire body at this time... Gently move your fingers and toes and enjoy this relaxed state.

Autogenic Training

Sit or lie down in a comfortable position. Close your eyes, take a couple of deep breaths, and focus your attention on the muscles throughout your body. As you discover tension, let it drain out of your body. Throughout this exercise you will be asked to focus on the bodily sensations of warmth and heaviness. These feelings occur when the body is relaxed and comfortable. Begin by focusing your attention on your head... (pause for 2 or 3 seconds with each...) With each breath your head becomes heavier... heavier... heavier... warmer... warmer... and warmer...

Now shift your focus to your arms and hands. With each breath your arms and hands become heavier... heavier... heavier... warmer... warmer and warmer... Now concentrate on your buttocks, legs, and feet. With each breath your buttocks, legs, and feet become heavier... heavier... heavier... warmer... warmer and warmer... Now as you relax, notice your torso becoming heavier... heavier... heavier... warmer... warmer and warmer... Now be aware of your entire body as it becomes heavier... heavier... heavier... warmer... warmer and warmer... Feel how heavy your entire body has become and notice the warmth you experience as you enjoy this state of relaxation and peacefulness.

The breathing and muscle relaxation exercises listed above have all been adapted from exercises found in *The Relaxation & Stress Reduction Workbook*[8] written by Martha Davis, Elizabeth Robbins Eshelman, and Matthew McKay. In each exercise, I begin by having athletes sit or lie in a comfortable position, close their eyes, and take a few deep breaths. I do this for a few reasons. First, it provides a good transition into the relaxation exercises. Second, sitting or lying can have an immediate impact on an over-activated body. Those positions, as well as the closing of one's eyes and deep breathing, are consistent with relaxation and rest. By closing their eyes, athletes are also able to eliminate visual stimuli that could be distracting. Finally, I want to condition athletes to relax by simply closing their eyes and taking a couple of deep breaths. This will be useful in actual performance situations where they might have only a few seconds to adjust their activation level. This conditioning will occur with repeated practice of the exercises to reduce stress and manage pre-competition over-activation. The exercises above can be read onto a cassette tape that can be used to guide you as you learn how to relax.

Every athlete differs in how they handle over-activation. The exercises described above have been very helpful for many athletes I have worked with professionally. Other methods athletes tend to use to help them relax include prayer, talking to others, smiling and laughing, listening to music, and imagery. The key is to find something that works for you, practice it regularly, and then use it as needed to bring about a "relaxation response."

journal exercise 15

Which relaxation exercise might you use in preparation for performance? When might it be most helpful to you? Practice it for a few days and write about your experience.

photo courtesy of Maggie Chan-Roper

ENERGIZE – "FIRE-UP"

There are two scenarios when athletes tend to be under-activated and come out playing flat. The first is at practice. If you compete in athletics for any length of time, you are going to have those days where you are tired, sore, unmotivated, discouraged, or focused on other aspects of your life besides your sport. I remember on many occasions as a basketball player when I would show up to practice flat and less than enthused to be there. To make matters worse, practice was held in the late afternoon when my activation level was already low. The second situation in which athletes often experience under-activation is competition against a weaker opponent. These are those games where your talent is superior to those you are competing against, and all you have to do is show up and have an average performance and you will win.

In these situations, it is important to have some strategies to help you get activated so you can perform your best. Signs of under-activation include a slowed heart rate, lethargy, fatigue, and lack of motivation and excitement. Like other problems that have already been discussed, the first step is to recognize that you are under-activated. There must also be desire on the part of the athlete to change their readiness to play. Some athletes choose not to make the attempt to change their activation level because it is "just practice" or a "meaningless game." The danger in such thinking is that bad habits can be developed and athletes can become more susceptible to injury when they are under-activated and unfocused. Most great athletes take pride in bringing their best everyday. This, too, becomes a habit and is part of their greatness.

There are a number of different strategies under-activated athletes can use to fire-up for performance. First, athletes need to be aware of their self-talk and how it impacts their energy level. For example, a swimmer might walk out onto the pool deck before practice and say, "Man, I don't want to be here today. I'm tired and sore. This is such a drag. There is no way I can make it through the workout today!" Obviously, this type of self-talk is only going to make the situation worse. It will leave the athlete feeling unmotivated and tired. Compare that situation with the following self-talk: "I'm pretty tired, but I need to get my energy level up for practice. I've made it through days like this before. I just need to get moving and stay positive and focused and I can have a good workout." Another strategy that can be useful is to physically move around. Remember, some of the signs of activation include an increase in heart and respiration rate and sweating. A vigorous physical warm-up can make a big difference in preparing an athlete to get off to a good start in practice and games.

Other mental strategies include energizing breathing, imagery, and cue words. Picture an Olympic weightlifter just prior to his lift. What does he do? First, he seems to shift his focus internal in his last few minutes of preparation. I have witnessed many weightlifters who close their eyes to imagine themselves successfully executing the lift. They then get all chalked up while they are talking to themselves. I do not know exactly what they are saying, but it is something that gets them charged up. Finally, just prior to their lift they begin taking short, rapid breaths as they focus in on the weight. Even the casual observer can witness the surge of energy experienced by the weightlifters as they go through their pre-lift routines.

All athletes can learn from this example. Rapid breathing for short

periods of time can boost energy, especially when paired with energizing cue words such as, "explode," "attack," and "dominate." Athletes can also imagine energy flowing into their body with each breath providing more strength, power, and endurance. There is also great power in positive imagery in which athletes see and feel themselves performing with energy, focus, and determination. Sometimes athletes must remind themselves why they are there in the first place. If they are unmotivated because it is only practice, they can become motivated by remembering their long-term goals. Focusing on outcome goals can help fuel athletes when they are feeling flat. They can also remind themselves their competitors have the same types of days and make a commitment to be more resilient than their peers.

Finally, external resources can help athletes deal with under-activation such as motivational tapes and speakers, upbeat music, supportive teammates and coaches, and inspirational highlights or movies. Many coaches do not want to rely too much on external sources of motivation. I believe it can be over done and lose its effectiveness, but when used selectively and timed appropriately, external motivation can make a big difference in activation, emotion, and focus.

journal exercise 16

When are you most likely to be under-activated? What have you done in the past to deal with this problem? Pick an energizing strategy discussed in this section and try it out this week at practice. Share your experience.

FOCUS PLAN

My son and I are learning how to play golf together. After hacking my way around the golf course a few times a summer for many years, I finally decided to take on the challenge of improving my game. My son attended a summer golf camp and we began reading and discussing how to better our swings. One time we played he really struggled with his swing. I noticed that he was taking his eyes off of the ball on his back swing, holding his club too tight, and not aligning his body properly to the hole when addressing his ball. I told him what I observed and we made a focus plan. On each shot I would stand behind him and help him line up with the hole properly. He would then have two simple reminders before beginning his swing, "Soft hands" and "See the ball." This is an example of a focus plan. There are many things he could focus on to improve his swing, but for that round he chose to focus only on those three areas. The focus plan kept it simple and his performance greatly improved.

A focus plan is nothing more than a conscious decision about what you choose to focus on for the game or practice. It should be simple and specific. However, it does requires planning on your part before you begin playing. Focus planning actually begins immediately following your previous performance or practice by asking yourself, "What do I need to do better tomorrow to improve?" Regular communication with a coach can be invaluable in helping you establish a focus plan. I recommend targeting only two or three goals at the most. Otherwise, your focus becomes too broad and you will defeat the whole purpose of this strategy.

Once you have picked your areas of focus, you need to commit yourself to doing it. You can strengthen your commitment by writing it down before practice on a 3 X 5 card or sharing your plan with a coach or teammate. Another helpful way to lock-in your plan is to spend a few minutes prior to the game or practice imagining what you plan to do.

A focus plan can include concentrating on anything that will improve your performance. It could be a technical aspect of performance, a tactical or strategic focus, or even an attitude. A national champion runner I worked with liked to remind herself to "run tall" as she neared the end of races. This helped her run more efficiently and with better form. I often had my best shooting games as a basketball player when I had a simple focus such as "smooth" or had my best rebounding games when I would focus on "dominate the boards." As you may have noticed, the use of cue words is often a part of a focus plan. Cue words keep the focus plan simple, which is important. Other examples of cue words include "explode," "quick feet," "next point," " be decisive," "attack," and "flow." Cue words and imagery are two simple ways to condense the focus plan into a powerful mental program that can be experienced in the mind and body before you even enter the athletic arena. They help create a mental blueprint that improves the likelihood of actualizing your plan. Cue words also serve as quick, easy reminders during your performance. Thus, a focus plan is a type of goal-setting strategy that targets specific areas of performance for a given practice or competition.

journal exercise **17**

Write your focus plan for an upcoming competition or practice. After the game or practice, evaluate how well you carried out your plan.

PERFORMANCE ROUTINES

One of my favorite books on mental training is *Heads-Up Baseball: Playing the Game One Pitch at a Time*,[9] which was written by Ken Ravizza and Tom Hanson. Much of what I write in this section has been influenced from their writings on performance routines in baseball. I strongly encourage athletes to develop performance routines they can consistently use as they prepare for practice and competition. The purpose of a performance routine is to get athletes ready to play by creating the proper activation level, emotional state, and focus. A good routine generally includes using a combination of mental training tools discussed in this chapter. Routines need to be flexible and may be changed as athletes mature and learn new ideas.

There is a difference between superstitious rituals and performance routines. Some athletes end up being slaves to rituals that may have little or no impact on how they perform. These rituals might include dressing a certain way, eating the same pre-game meal, or listening to the right song. Sometimes athletes get so extreme they become excessively anxious if their ritual is disrupted in any way. This can obviously have a negative impact on how they perform. However, there is a fine line between a well-developed performance routine and a superstitious ritual, especially since many routines become highly ritualized. A good routine should be simple and straightforward. Each athlete needs to find what works best for them. I encourage athletes to choose activities they can control, to have a clear rationale for each step in the routine, and develop a routine that is replicable across performance settings. Sometimes athletes have a tough time letting go of some superstitious behaviors. In these cases, it might be best to continue certain quirky behaviors and traditions as long as they do not interfere with performance.

A good performance routine has a defined starting point when the athlete begins his or her preparation. It is often helpful to have a specific transition point identified. For instance, preparation for practice might begin when an athlete enters the locker room. Preparation for competition could begin at dinner the night before the game. It does not matter when it begins, but it is helpful to choose a starting point when you say, "Okay, it's now time to start getting myself ready to play." From that point on, there needs to be a funneling process in which athletes narrow their focus and engage in activities that prepare both the mind and body to perform. I will illustrate this process in the following examples of a pre-practice and a pre-competition routine.

In my experience with collegiate athletes, very few have consistent pre-practice routines. The time demands are such that it is hard to find the time

PRE-PRACTICE
ROUTINE

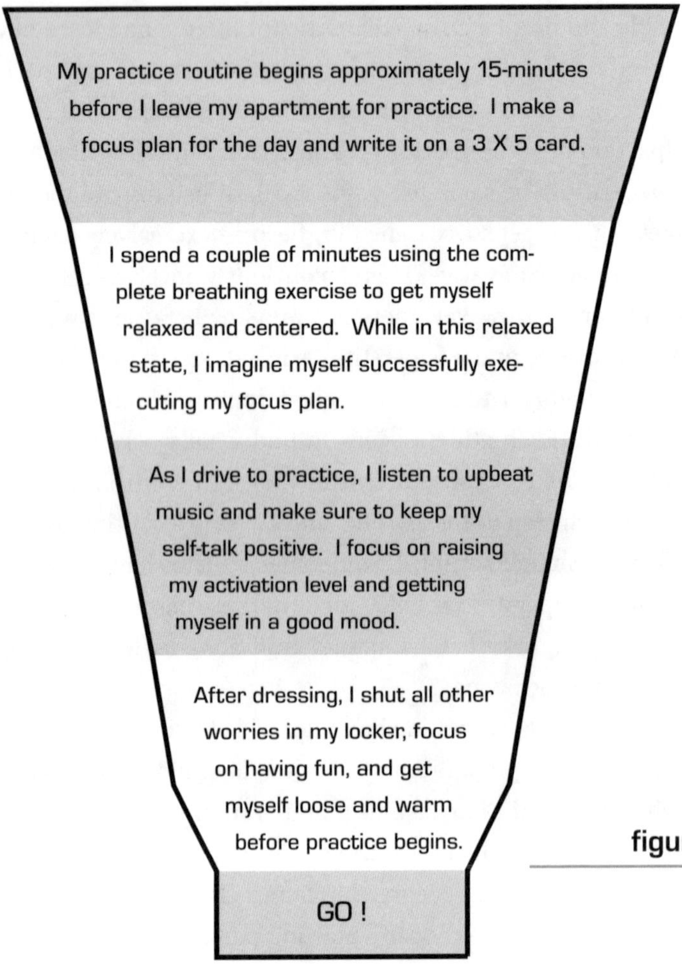

My practice routine begins approximately 15-minutes before I leave my apartment for practice. I make a focus plan for the day and write it on a 3 X 5 card.

I spend a couple of minutes using the complete breathing exercise to get myself relaxed and centered. While in this relaxed state, I imagine myself successfully executing my focus plan.

As I drive to practice, I listen to upbeat music and make sure to keep my self-talk positive. I focus on raising my activation level and getting myself in a good mood.

After dressing, I shut all other worries in my locker, focus on having fun, and get myself loose and warm before practice begins.

GO !

figure **5**

to do much mental preparation prior to practice. However, the pre-practice routine outlined in figure 5 does not take a lot of extra time. Some coaches I have consulted with take a few minutes right at the beginning of practice to have their athletes set a few practice goals, share them with a teammate, and image themselves successfully executing their plan. They also have their athletes follow-up with each other after practice. I call this "practicing with a purpose." The main point with the pre-practice routine is to take just a few minutes and do something to get yourself ready to play.

In contrast to pre-practice routines, pre-competition plans are commonly used by athletes. Figure 6 follows a format I like to use in my consultation with athletes. There are four phases to the plan: the night before competition, the morning of the performance, the last few hours before "show time," and those last couple of minutes of mental preparation. The night before the performance is a great time to review your focus plan for the upcoming competition. It is also a good time to relax and fill your mind with positive thoughts and images. A good imagery session the night before

can help tie things together for the next day. From that point on, athletes need to do less thinking and more trusting. The next morning might include an imagery session, but much of the preparation time should be spent managing the activation level for the day and creating a positive emotional state. There is a lot of variability among athletes in how they like to

PRE-COMPETITION
ROUTINE

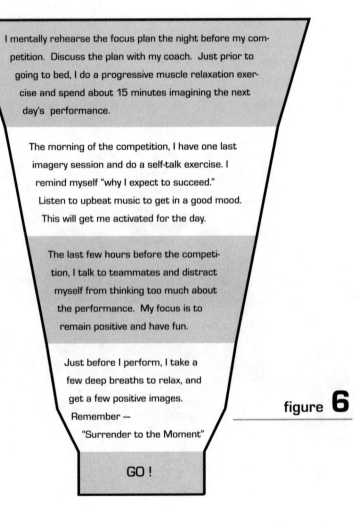

I mentally rehearse the focus plan the night before my competition. Discuss the plan with my coach. Just prior to going to bed, I do a progressive muscle relaxation exercise and spend about 15 minutes imagining the next day's performance.

The morning of the competition, I have one last imagery session and do a self-talk exercise. I remind myself "why I expect to succeed." Listen to upbeat music to get in a good mood. This will get me activated for the day.

The last few hours before the competition, I talk to teammates and distract myself from thinking too much about the performance. My focus is to remain positive and have fun.

Just before I perform, I take a few deep breaths to relax, and get a few positive images. Remember — "Surrender to the Moment"

GO !

figure **6**

handle the last few hours before they compete. Some athletes get quiet and introspective and spend some time deep breathing, imaging, and reviewing their game plan. Others like to get outside of their head and distract themselves from thinking too much. They may talk and laugh with teammates, read a book, play video games, or watch television. Finally, those last few minutes are usually spent managing activation and dealing with the emotions of the moment. I have noticed that many of the best performances occur when athletes surrender to the moment and simply trust their preparation. Their self-talk generally goes something like this, "Well, it's time to do it! You're ready! Just trust and let it happen!"

journal exercise 18

Draw two funnels. Then write a personalized pre-practice and pre-competition routine. Make it something that works for you. You can think back to past performances where you excelled for ideas. Practice your routines and revise them as needed.

COPING ROUTINE

A coping routine is similar to a focus plan. It is designed to help athletes refocus during a performance when they get over-activated, emotionally upset, or distracted. Experienced athletes can generally tell you what types of things get them off-track when they are performing. Maybe it is a bad call from an official, poor weather conditions, a stupid mistake on their part, or a competitors trash-talking. It does not matter what it is. What is important is for athletes to know what pushes their buttons and ultimately causes them to lose focus. The coping routine is thought out well in advance and is rehearsed mentally so it becomes available when needed during competition.

A good coping routine includes a combination of taking a deep breath, using positive self-talk, and "letting go" of the source of the distraction by refocusing on the present. A tennis player I worked with would fall apart when her opponent would make a bad call. She hated conflict and would avoid challenging her opponent on the call. Instead, she would get "upset inside" and lose several points in a row. Sometimes the momentum change would be so drastic that it would determine the outcome of the match. We developed a coping plan that included the following routine. As soon as she was aware she was upset and losing control, she would take a deep breath, slowly walk to the back fence, pick up her towel and dry off her face, drop the towel while saying to herself "let it go," walk back to the court with a quicker pace while rehearsing her mental strategy and giving herself an instructional cue.

The deep breath is her signal to relax and regain control. The slow walk to the fence gives her time to release some pent up emotions, identify what she needs to do differently, and take control of the pace of the match. Drying off her face and dropping the towel is symbolic of wiping away the past and letting it go. When she is real frustrated she may throw the towel down with a little extra energy and determination, but without being unsportsmanlike and letting her opponent know she is frustrated. Her walk back is quicker and more consistent with her normal pace. This is a signal she is ready to get back in the match. The cue word or rehearsal of her mental strategy puts her right back in the present. This whole routine may take 10-15 seconds and is only used when she recognizes she needs to regain control of herself and change the momentum of the match. Coping routines can be very helpful and should fit within the flow of the game. A good coping routine will generally impact an athlete's activation level and emotional state, and help to regain a competitive focus.

journal exercise **19**

Identify situations in your sport that negatively impact your readiness level. Write down a coping strategy that might help you deal better with these situations in the future. Image your coping plan before using it at practice or in competition.

chapter 5

application to life outside of sports

"I'm a great believer in luck, and
I find the harder I work, the
more I have of it."
– Thomas Jefferson

I n the previous chapters, I have focused on teaching athletes how to achieve higher levels of success in their sport. There have been three main areas addressed. First, I outlined the building blocks for success. I described in detail the importance of having big dreams and believing in yourself. These building blocks are the foundation to any success. Once those building blocks are in place, athletes must develop a plan of attack and commit themselves to their plan through hard work and sacrifice to realize their dreams. The final building block that ties everything together is living a disciplined lifestyle on a consistent basis. These building blocks can be thought of as a recipe for success.

In the third chapter, I focused on readiness to perform. There are three keys to readiness. They include getting the body properly activated, managing emotion, and focusing on the right cues at the time of performance. In chapter four, I described some mental training tools that directly impact activation, emotion, and focus. Athletes can greatly benefit from the mental programming that takes place through positive self-talk and imagery. Furthermore, they can prepare for performance by using relaxation exercises to calm down, energizing strategies to fire-up, and focusing plans to reduce potential distractions. Finally, I recommended athletes use pre-performance routines in which they can integrate the mental training tools and use them in a systematic way that improves the likelihood of consistent, high-level performance.

Athletics gives student-athletes the opportunity to develop skills and attributes that will help them succeed in other areas of their life. These other areas include, but are not limited to, academics, career, and relationships. In this final chapter, I will briefly explain how the mental training tools discussed in this book can be applied to these areas of life.

I have watched many athletes transition from their sport during the last several years. Those who make successful transitions have prepared themselves well during their playing days by getting a good education and having a vision of what they want to do when their athletic career is over. They have career dreams and seek for balance in their lives by taking full advantage of their educational opportunities and establishing good relationships with others. They also have a broad identity and refuse to accept the limited role others want to place on them. They are not just "jocks." They believe in themselves and fully expect to excel in the classroom, in their relationships with others, and in their future careers. They back up this belief by disciplining their lives, having goals, making sacrifices, and working hard to be successful.

Those who have struggled to transition well from their sport fail to plan well for their future. In many cases, they have difficulty seeing themselves succeed at anything except their sport. I have heard many athletes say, "My sport is all I know how to do. I've focused my whole life on being the best athlete I could be and lack the ability to do anything else." Without dreams and a belief in themselves, they become frightened when their playing days end. Unfortunately, fear paralyzes people and keeps them stuck. Athletes who struggle with these issues need assistance and help in understanding they can make a significant contribution within their family relationships and in their communities. However, they must first return to the basics and start dreaming and believing in themselves. From their dreams they can commit themselves to a plan of attack and go to work. Successful athletes have already learned how to work hard, are willing to make sacrifices, and can be quite disciplined as they pursue important goals. This process is no different than athletics. As they begin to have some small successes, their confidence will grow. Their belief in themselves will free them from the fear that initially held them back from taking the risks necessary for growth. Thus, the building blocks for success certainly apply to these other areas of life.

I would like to conclude the book by sharing how I personally use the mental training tools in my daily life. I find it a challenge to manage my activation level, emotions, and to regularly live in the present by staying focused. The tools discussed in chapter four have been valuable in all areas of my life.

I graduated in 1989 from Mesa State College and finished my eligibility as a college basketball player. The transition from college basketball was difficult, especially the first year after graduation. However, I was blessed with the opportunity to pursue a graduate degree in psychology. My dream then changed from athletics to graduating with a doctoral degree in the field I love. I was confident I could succeed because I had done well in school as an undergraduate student. However, the six years it took me to get through graduate school were some of the most challenging of my life. To juggle the demands of the heavy academic load, a growing young family, and a job seemed overwhelming at times. I made it through because of a loving Heavenly Father, a good support network of family and friends, and the use of many of the mental training tools described in this book.

I had a plan of attack I reviewed often and regularly talked about with my dear wife. The road to graduation was long and hard and I never would have made it had I not broken down the long-term goal into manageable steps that could be taken daily. I relied heavily on taking things one semester at a time and broke the semester down into a weekly goals. Each Sunday

I would review my progress and then set new goals for the week. That made my daily life easier because all I needed to do was follow the weekly plan each day. My confidence grew with each passing week and semester as I had success. Thus, regular goal-setting was instrumental in getting me through.

Controlling my self-talk was also important. Any journey is going to have some difficult times. I recall a couple of times when I thought I would need to quit school due to finances, illness and death in our family, and because the academic load seemed too heavy to bear. What got me through was simple self-talk statements like, "Hang in there, you can do it." "Your family has sacrificed too much to quit now." "If others can do it, why not you." There is great power in using self-talk that leads to optimism, resiliency, and determination. Sometimes my self-talk was negative and self-defeating, but I was surrounded by people who would provide the positive encouragement when I needed it most.

I also recall a time when I was struggling to get my dissertation completed. I was discouraged and sitting in the office of a psychologist at the counseling center where I worked. We shared her office to meet with our clients. She had graduated from the same graduate program in which I was a student. On her office wall was a framed copy of her diploma. I had a few minutes before my next client would arrive for counseling. I remember sitting back in the chair and using imagery in which I experienced myself completing my academic goals. I visualized myself typing my dissertation at my computer. My thoughts were clear and I typed quickly. Then, I imagined myself meeting with my dissertation committee to defend what I had researched and written. In that meeting, I was confident and communicated clearly and assertively. I then experienced the thrill of having them sign my final copy of the dissertation and imagined what it was going to be like to walk out of the library having turned in my dissertation to be bound in to a book. Finally, I mentally experienced my graduation day as I shared that thrill with my family and thanked them for their support. When I finished my imagery experience, I felt excited and motivated to finish my dissertation so I could graduate. For the next 10 weeks, I regularly used imagery to help me finish my dissertation. I used the same psychologist's office each

week and would use her framed diploma as my cue to visualize myself fulfilling my dreams. Many of my actual experiences upon completion of my dissertation were eerily similar to my imagery. I am convinced there is great power in programming the mind with positive self-talk and images.

Another skill I regularly use is focus planning. Each morning I have a routine which includes prayer, scripture study, and exercise. I have found it extremely helpful to have a focus plan for the day. What I choose to focus on changes based upon what I want to work on that day. Sometimes I need to focus on being more kind to my wife and children and managing my emotions better. Other days it may be carrying myself with confidence as I teach a class or effectively making a presentation at work. It generally depends upon what I have that day or making an adjustment on something I could do better in my life. My focus planning includes picking one or two things I want to focus on during the day. I then pray for help to accomplish my plan. Upon completion of my prayer I will take a minute or two and visualize myself having success with my plan. In some cases, I will also share my plan with my wife and ask for her help, especially if it involves being a better father or husband. The whole process takes only a few minutes, but has a profound impact on my personal growth and development. The days I have a focus plan I am better able to concentrate on what I am doing.

Another set of tools I consistently use are energizing and relaxation exercises. Before a class or meeting that I am stressed about I will often get comfortable, close my eyes, and do a few minutes of deep breathing. I have used relaxation exercises regularly enough that I can close my eyes and take a few deep breaths while saying "relax" and get a good relaxation response. This skill has also been very helpful when dealing with my children. I have a tendency to lose my temper and this skill has helped me manage both my activation level and emotions. It also helps me get centered and focus before giving a presentation at work. I also use the energizing techniques described in chapter four to get my energy level up early in the morning and late afternoon when my energy level wanes. The most helpful energizing techniques for me have been pairing physical movement with energizing self-talk and rapid, deep breathing.

Finally, let me discuss the importance of having a daily routine.

Throughout the book I have emphasized the importance of athletes getting themselves properly activated, in the right emotional state, and focused on the task at hand. I have personally found this to be equally important to function well at work and at home with my family. If I consistently adhere to my morning routine of prayer, scripture study, focus planning, and exercise, I function better throughout the day. I feel ready to play for that day. Now, having said that, I do not want to give the impression that I perform this routine every day. Life sometimes gets in the way of my plans. Some change and variability keeps life interesting and exciting. I look forward to vacations and weekends because they are natural breaks from day-to-day life. However, when I am in my regular work schedule, my daily morning routine is as important to me as an athlete's pre-competition routine. It gets me ready to perform my best for that day. Every day we get new opportunities to perform so we might as well seek to be our best. Find something that works for you and do it!

CONCLUSION

Well, that's it! This has been my best attempt to share what I have learned about performance enhancement through my experiences as a student-athlete and sport psychologist. My purpose in writing this book was to provide meaningful information about what it takes for student-athletes to perform at a consistently high level and share it in a manner that is simple to understand and practical to use. There are certainly resources available that are more comprehensive and describe mental training in greater detail. However, it is my hope that student-athletes will use this book to better understand themselves as performers and refer to it often for reminders that will lead them to success and prepare them for performance. One final reminder: those who are prepared deserve the right to excel. So, dream big, believe in yourself, stay committed, and work hard. Be disciplined in your approach to school, athletics, and life. Then, use the tools you learned in this book to get yourself ready to play each and every time you perform. Trust yourself and have fun! That is what sports and life are all about.

REFERENCES AND SUGGESTED READINGS

1   Rotella, R. (1995). *Golf is Not a Game of Perfect.* New York: Simon & Schuster.

2   Pitino, R. (1997). *Success is a Choice.* New York: Broadway Books.

3   Loehr, J. E. (1994). *The New Toughness Training for Sports.* New York: Penguin Books.

4   Peck, M.S. (1978). *The Road Less Traveled.* New York: Simon & Schuster.

5   Bell, K.F. (1982). *Winning Isn't Normal.* Austin, TX: Keel Publications.

6   Hanin, Y.L. (Ed.) (2000). *Emotions in Sport.* Champaign, IL: Human Kinetics.

7   Nideffer, R.M. (1985). *Athletes' Guide to Mental Training.* Champaign, IL: Human Kinetics.

8   Davis, M., Eshelman, E.R., McKay, M. (1995). *The Relaxation and Stress Reduction Workbook.* Oakland, CA: New Harbinger.

9   Ravizza, K., & Hanson, Tom. (1995). *Heads-up Baseball: Playing the Game One Pitch at a Time.* Lincolnwood, IL: Contemporary Books.

To order additional copies of...

READY TO PLAY
mental training for student-athletes

Ron Chamberlain, Ph.D.

Send your name and mailing address, along with a check or money order to:

- Ready to Play
  1133 Columbia Lane
  Provo, UT 84604

- Charge to Credit Card:
  1-877-845-3592 or
  www.thepsychologyofsports.com

- Cost per book:

	price	quantity	Total
	$12.95	_____	_____
shipping $3 first book		1	$3.00
$1 each additional copy		_____	_____
Sales Tax 6.25% (Utah only)			_____
GRAND TOTAL			_____